# UNHAPPY HOLIDAYS

AN ADVENT DEVOTIONAL

# UNHAPPY HOLIDAYS

## BLESSINGS FOR A BLUE CHRISTMAS

SHERAH-LEIGH GERBER

Harrisonburg, Virginia

Herald Press
PO Box 866, Harrisonburg, Virginia 22803
www.HeraldPress.com

Library of Congress Cataloging-in-Publication Data
Names: Gerber, Sherah-Leigh author
Title: Unhappy holidays : blessings for a blue Christmas (an advent devotional) / Sherah-Leigh Gerber.
Description: Harrisonburg, Virginia : Herald Press, [2025] | Includes bibliographical references.
Identifiers: LCCN 2025018284 (print) | LCCN 2025018285 (ebook) | ISBN 9781513816470 paperback | ISBN 9781513816487 ebook
Subjects: LCSH: Advent--Prayers and devotions | Christmas--Prayers and devotions | Devotional calendars--Mennonites | BISAC: RELIGION / Holidays / Christmas & Advent | RELIGION / Christian Living / Spiritual Growth | LCGFT: Devotional literature | Prayers
Classification: LCC BV40 .G474 2025 (print) | LCC BV40 (ebook) | DDC 242/.332--dc23/eng/20250820
LC record available at https://lccn.loc.gov/2025018284
LC ebook record available at https://lccn.loc.gov/2025018285

Study guides are available for many Herald Press titles at www.HeraldPress.com.

UNHAPPY HOLIDAYS

Library of Congress Control Number: 2025018284
International Standard Book Number: 978-1-5138-1647-0 (paperback); 978-1-5138-1648-7 (ebook)
Printed in United States of America



29 28 27 26 25 10 9 8 7 6 5 4 3 2 1

*For those who have navigated unchosen journeys or a dark night of the soul.*

*May you sense the nearness of God.*

# CONTENTS



## DAILY DEVOTIONALS

## BONUS MATERIALS

# INTRODUCTION

In an Advent sermon on hope, the preacher began with examples of things we wait for: a baby to be born, test results, voting outcomes, the storm to pass. I leaned forward in the pew, reaching for my bag. In the bottom, I found a crumpled receipt and uncapped pen. Using the back of the hymnal as a makeshift lap desk, I scratched out my grumble of a response.

*What about the things we wait for with no guaranteed resolution, change, or outcome? Not everything we wait for comes to be. How do we wait for the unknown?*

As a spiritual director, caregiver coach, and former pastor, I know all too well that the experiences and questions that bring people before God are less often those of hope and joy and more often because of loss and desperation. The gap between what is professed or preached and our spiritual need is often wide. As a result, the holiday season can be a particularly tender time when our experience is out of sync with the good tidings and great joy of the Christmas message.

In these soul care spaces, you become aware of the hardships and griefs that those in your community carry. The pastor is often the first call when tragedy strikes—a diagnosis, a divorce, a death. Then last to receive word of a celebration or good news. It truly is a sacred privilege to hold space with people, an honor to be invited into those most tender times. Bearing witness to the hard and holy soul work, having a front-row seat to transformation and God's miraculous intervention is thrilling.

But every time I prepare to preach a message, write a note of care, or offer a prayer, the faces of those in the bleakness of a midwinter journey of their soul come to mind. Is this still true? Is this really good news to those within my community who are hurting? To those awaiting a miracle? To those wondering where God is?

I have always loved this time of year. I believe the seasons of Advent and Christmastide are rich with opportunities for spiritual connection. And I know that it can be a particularly painful stretch of days for those who are experiencing loss and grief. While the traditional themes of love, joy, peace, and hope are heralded in worship, Advent is a season of waiting. It acknowledges that faith requires holding on to hope, trusting in what is yet to be while living in the mess and pain of our present moment.

While Advent is for all of us, it is particularly for those who have questions, for those with need, and for those sitting in darkness. Advent is a time when we offer our experiences before God. We remember and celebrate God's faithful action in the past as we await the arrival of the light and anticipate transformation in our own situations and circumstances.

Whether you are grieving or waiting for something with little hope of resolution, no guarantee of healing, or assurance of what is to come, Advent is the season for you. For out of chaos God creates, and into darkness the light shines. It is in the silence that the Word arrives, and out of death that resurrection comes. Thanks be to God.

## ORIENTATION TO ADVENT

As a young adult, my mother spent time living and working in Germany and Switzerland. There she was introduced to the tradition of the Advent wreath. Shaped by this meaningful practice, she committed to a household tradition of candle lighting to mark the weeks of Advent. I have wholeheartedly embraced my mother's love for Advent and Christmas traditions. I now have a bookshelf of Advent resources that I have collected over the years. I have my favorite readings that I return to time and again.

While it is more commonplace now for Christians across the spectrum of denominations to celebrate the season of Advent, this stretch of weeks with candle lightings and purple and pink vestments is rooted in longstanding liturgical tradition. The Catholic Church along with Anglican, Episcopal, and Orthodox communities, among others, worship with an emphasis on ritual and sacraments, which is sometimes referred to as the "high church" tradition. While other Protestant faith expressions have typically distanced themselves from these practices, elements of the structured rituals and rhythms of the church year are a part of the worship life of many congregations.

Growing up in a Mennonite home as the child of two pastors, and having worked as a pastor myself, the Christmas season holds a mix of emotions for me. I love the various traditions, the music, the evergreens, and the warm glow of Christmas lights. But I also feel the weight of managing frenetic schedules, coordinating extra services and programs, and holding space for others to experience the good news of the season. Just as being the parent responsible for creating Christmas magic at home can negatively impact the holiday season, so too preparing for and leading in this sacred season can dampen the good tidings of great joy for church leaders.

And so, Advent has become more significant to me, because I have come to see it as an opportunity to explore the gifts of wintering, especially for those of us in the Northern Hemisphere. The gift of God's good creation reminds us that for everything there is a season. Fallow times are as integral to fruitfulness as seedtime and harvest. Though it may be invisible or below the surface, work is happening underground, quietly, in the dark. So, too, our souls experience these winter seasons. Through our experiences of rest, renewal, and hidden transformation, what once might have been unimaginable or impossible takes root in the long night.

Instead of something to be dreaded or feared, the additional hours of darkness that mark our days as we move toward the longest night, so near to the celebration of the nativity, have much to offer us as well. Advent is a chance to accept the invitation of the darkness. While unchosen events and grief may initially feel like a barrier to faith, sometimes being plunged into the dark is really an invitation to rest. This is an opportunity to allow things to surface that will be instructive, that need to be considered, and that will ultimately teach us to navigate the next stage of our journey.

At this time of year, Advent is an opportunity to prepare our hearts and minds to once again receive Jesus. We are invited to notice the ways that God is with us. We consider what it means to prepare for the second Advent, offering our laments and longings as we anticipate the fullness of God's shalom in Christ's second coming.

## A WORD ON BLESSING

Once a month, I lead group spiritual direction sessions at a local counseling center. This is a benefit the organization offers its employees, an opportunity to do some soul care in the midst of emotionally and spiritually demanding work. Drawing on the lectionary text for the week, we spend time together reading and reflecting on Scripture, concluding with a blessing based on the passage.

These kinds of blessings are at the heart of this book. The words of invocation are offerings of care and courage for you as you navigate all that the Advent season holds. The act of blessing is a way of recognizing sacredness. It is a way of inviting God into all that is unfolding, into our experience both in pain and petition. As spiritual writer Christine Valters Paintner reflected in one of her daily email meditations, "The act of blessing is a really special way of paying attention. . . . It is an act of consecrating time."[1]

The daily blessings are an offering of words for when you may not have them. These are my prayers for you, a claim of hope in the bleak midwinter. Each blessing is a recognition that all parts of our lives have a place in God's story.

## HOW TO USE THIS BOOK

This book of reflections and blessings was created to be a daily guide, a gentle companion, through the days of December.

You may already have a designated time in your day for prayerful reflection. Maybe you will make space for these readings as a new rhythm in Advent. Or perhaps you will read through this devotional in fits and starts, catching up on a week's worth of reflections on a Sunday afternoon or skimming through and looking for blessings that catch your eye. There is no wrong way to move through this book or engage the Advent season. This is an invitation (or permission for those who may need it) to pay attention to what your soul is longing for at this time.

The scriptures selected for the month are drawn from Wilda Gafney's work on a reimagined lectionary that centers stories of women. Gafney's selections, translations, and interpretations in *A Women's Lectionary for the Whole Church (Year A)* and *A Women's Lectionary for the Whole Church (Year W)* consider the perspectives and voices of those who are often marginalized or erased from Scripture. Her work draws from the rabbinic tradition of midrash and contemporary practice of sanctified imagination along with her close reading of the sacred texts.[2] The primary principles of Gafney's work resonate with the core values of the Anabaptist tradition, of which I'm part. Our tradition emphasizes the priesthood of all believers, reading the Bible and interpreting Scripture with a community lens, and honoring the insights and experiences of the gathered group.

The structure of the seasons and celebrations of the liturgical year may be unfamiliar to those of us from "low church" traditions, and the use of lectionary may also be new. Formed as a way to move systematically and intentionally through the Bible, the lectionary was created as a three-year cycle of scripture texts for congregational use. Each week consists of four readings, a selection from the Hebrew Scriptures, a psalm, a gospel reading, and a portion from a New Testament epistle.

More recently, a variety of lectionaries have emerged, including the Narrative Lectionary and Gafney's offering.

You may wish to read this book with your Bible open, as the included lines of scripture are just a few key verses from the larger lectionary passages for the week. While the texts of the Christmas story may be familiar to you, sometimes seeing the context of the focus verses brings new insights and ideas.

The additional materials at the end of this book are resources to adapt the devotionals for households, for small groups, or for use in corporate worship. This is one way you may lead or share the Advent journey with others.

# INVITATION

In 2019, on Memorial Day weekend, we had loaded our two little children into our car for the seven-hour drive over the mountains toward my husband's childhood home. It was a quiet ride as we tried to prepare ourselves for what was to come. That morning, my in-laws received confirmation of our whispered fears. My mother-in-law was suffering from amyotrophic lateral sclerosis (ALS), more commonly known as Lou Gehrig's disease.

Six months later, I sat at my desk in the church office, struggling to craft words that would welcome the congregation into the Advent season. I was weary from our monthly sojourns north, crammed in among our responsibilities of full-time work and parenting a first and third grader. Our hearts were breaking with anticipatory grief and the pain of watching a loved one suffer and decline.

Despite the doctors' earlier estimates, we now knew this would be our final holiday season together. After one last Christmas morning on the farm, we would move my mother-in-law into a facility where she could receive round-the-clock care as her body slowly shut down.

The cursor blinked on the blank page of my computer screen as Sunday morning drew nearer. Where was the comfort and joy? What words of hope and peace could I offer when my world didn't feel merry and bright? What does it mean to prepare and anticipate when the things we are awaiting are grievous and dreadful?

I have spent six Christmas seasons as a pastor, mediating the conflicts around when carols can begin to be sung in worship, crafting candle-lighting litanies, and googling simple crafts for kids in the ten minutes of response time after the sermon. I've negotiated with flower committees about Advent wreaths, nativities, and banners. And even though it was always a scramble to line up enough volunteers to usher or lead music in the busy weeks of family gatherings and travel plans, I had loved the rituals and traditions of the Advent season, the familiar hymns, candlelight, and themes of hope, love, joy, and peace that threaded through the month of December.

The liturgical calendar reminds us that as Christians we do not live on the world's time. The church has its own rhythms and rituals to nurture our souls along the discipleship journey and through the worship life of the community of God's people. The season of Advent invites us to a time of intentional preparation. In these weeks of waiting, we prepare to celebrate the incarnation, the birth of Jesus, just as we prepare for the second advent, the return of Christ.

So, I stood before my congregation on the first Sunday of Advent that year and said:

> *This morning, we light the first Advent candle, in anticipation of God's justice breaking in. God longs to free us from all that holds us captive to fear, confusion, and even despair. We light this candle as a reminder to take heart. God is coming to make things right.*

While I love much about this time of year (this is my second book focused on Advent!), the season is not really about designer Christmas trees, perfectly decorated sugar cookies, or a bevy of gifts in matching wrapping paper. If you love those things, that is fine! The nostalgia, joy of connecting to others, and favorite traditions have their place. But at the heart of Advent is an invitation to renew our commitments to the spiritual practices that form and inform our faith. It is the season for those of us who are weary, for those burdened by grief and loss as we are invited to make space in our hearts and minds to receive anew the many gifts of incarnation.

That last Christmas together, we lovingly placed our favorite ornaments on Grandma's tree as familiar carols played through the Bluetooth speaker. We reminisced as we unboxed each one, remembering the favorite vacation spot that this souvenir was from or which grandchild's fingerprints adorned the wobbly clay bell. We filled the kitchen with the scents of cinnamon and cloves, making small batches of our favorite cookies and Christmas candy to enjoy with mugs of hot chocolate as we watched *White Christmas*.

On Christmas morning, we read from the gospel of Luke, unwrapped gifts, and enjoyed cinnamon rolls. Laughter and tears mingled as we gave and received what would be our last gifts. We had a good, holy, and hard Christmas together.

## BLESSING FOR WHEN YOU MAY BE LIVING A NIGHTMARE

In the midst of the devastating and extraordinary,
may you have the strength to do the ordinary and daily.
When fear lodges in your throat—
when the monster of *what if* sits on your chest—
may you stay present to what is, without catastrophizing.

In the failure, disappointment, misunderstanding, and closed doors,
may hope slip between, a hedge of protection around your heart.
When you are holding onto the end of your rope—
when you cannot see a path forward, a way through—
may you refuse to assign meaning or outcomes in the
messy middle.

And in the heartbreaking pain of separation
and loss and grief and death (after death after death),
may you be held by the arms that are able to hold what
you cannot.

# DAILY DEVOTIONALS

*December 1*

# THE CHAOS OF THRESHOLDS

LECTIONARY READING: GENESIS 1:1–5

---

When God began to create the heavens and the earth, the earth was complete chaos, and darkness covered the face of the deep, while a wind from God swept over the face of the waters. Then God said, "Let there be light," and there was light. And God saw that the light was good, and God separated the light from the darkness. God called the light Day, and the darkness he called Night. And there was evening and there was morning, the first day. **(Genesis 1:1–5)**

---

Entering the 2020 holiday season, so much was in flux. It had been a difficult stretch between my mother-in-law's ALS diagnosis, decline, and death—all overlapping with a global pandemic. Everyone was navigating unprecedented times, and pastoring through the uncertainties of COVID was exhausting. As Advent approached, I had a semblance of peace; after more than a year of upheaval and grief, my husband and I had come to some clarity. We were on the cusp of significant change, on the threshold of something new. We were confident and unified in our direction, but the how of it all was yet to be revealed.

Thresholds are times pregnant with possibility and rife with uncertainty. Sometimes they are welcomed, even chosen, but sometimes we are forced to stand on the ledge and face the murkiness of the unknown.

Advent is a threshold season. The stretch between Thanksgiving (in the United States) and Christmas is a space of waiting. Thresholds can be exciting as one anticipates something new, a fresh start or a change in course, but thresholds can also be excruciating as the liminal space between what has been and what is yet to become drags on.

And so, thresholds can test us. They test the strength of our courage to move forward, to make a change, or to charge into something new and unknown. Our desire for control is revealed. There is only so much discomfort we can tolerate. Do we trust in the unfolding? And just how long must we wait for the new thing? Will it be an apocalypse, a dramatic unveiling or revealing of truth, or an epiphany of delightful revelation and insight?

We often think of the Christmas season as a time of good cheer, festive parties, thoughtful gifts, colorful lights, and holiday feasts. And it can be. Nostalgia-stirred childhood memories, as well as memories from when we created our own traditions, can warm our hearts during these weeks. Sometimes togetherness, activities, and connections with our past are welcome gifts in the dark of winter.

But what happens when the reality of life stands in stark contrast to these expectations? Strained family relationships or an empty nest can disrupt our vision for the perfect holiday celebration. Illness, divorce proceedings, and natural disasters do not care about the calendar. What are the gifts of the holiday season for the ones who are lonely, grieving, or hurting? Travel woes, splitting time, and political and budget differences can cause great distress within some of our closest relationships. How do we live into the spirit of the Christmas season when all is not merry and bright?

And then we remember that as it was in the beginning, it is out of chaos that God moves, animates, and creates (Genesis 1:1–3). When we come to the end of our resources and reconcile our expectations, we can begin to notice the divine presence. When the chaos of our lives overwhelms us, we wonder where God is. Yet as the opening lines of Scripture attest, God is present. God is hovering over the chaos. God is speaking, bringing light, order, and transformation. This is who God is.

No matter how you are coming to this season, Advent is for you. This is the season to name our longing for renewed hope and to practice trusting in what is unfolding. Through rituals that help us notice the growing light and God's presence with us through it all, we claim and proclaim that God is with us.

Whether in chaos or with longing, with a heart of eager anticipation or a soul heavy with dread, there are gifts and blessings to nurture and sustain your soul within this season of anticipation. The threshold of Advent is an invitation to step into a place of hope, where we believe that transformation is always possible and claim the promise of the already-and-not-yet reality of God's reign: things will not always be this way.

## BLESSING FOR THE CHAOS OF THRESHOLDS

May you dare to hope
  when you find yourself in darkness,
  staring down into the deep,
  facing the swirl of chaos.

May you have the courage to step up
  to the precipice, a threshold—
  to teeter on the edge.

May you dare to hope
  when you feel the sweep of the Wind,
  hear the whisper of the Divine,
  notice the pinprick of Light.

May you have the patience to
  sit in the before, on the threshold—
  holding on through the not-quite-yet.

May you dare to hope.
For in the
  wind and wave,
  darkness and light,
  chaos and order,
God has come.
And,
  God is not done.

*December 2*

# ALREADY AND NOT YET

LECTIONARY READING: 1 JOHN 3:1–3

---

See what love the Father has given us, that we should be called children of God, and that is what we are. The reason the world does not know us is that it did not know him. Beloved, we are God's children now; what we will be has not yet been revealed. **(1 John 3:1–2)**

---

One Advent, I came across a book written in collaboration between artist Emily McDowell and psychologist Kelsey Crowe entitled *There Is No Good Card for This*. It articulated something I felt so much of the time as I offered pastoral care to people in very challenging circumstances. Just as counselors and first responders need to find ways to leave the heavy things they bear witness to at the office (so to speak), part of embracing a pastoral identity meant wrestling with how to carry the griefs and concerns that were ever present.

I once heard the work of pastoral care likened to having a constant low-grade fever. One is ever aware of the heartbreaks, anxieties, and disappointments that people are carrying. It truly was my greatest privilege to journey with people through some of the most difficult seasons of their lives, to hold space for them to process, to hold on to hope when the light grew dim, and to bear witness to the ways that God was at work. But the reality remained—I more often got calls, texts, and emails with bad news. The heavy moments and points of desperation are when people reach out. Engagements, pregnancies, and promotions were much less likely to be shared or celebrated with me in my role as pastor.

Artist Emily McDowell is known for her greeting cards. Some of her most popular ones include *When life gives you lemons, I won't tell you a story about my cousin's friend who died of lemons.* And *I wish I could take away your pain. Or at least take away the people who compare it to the time their hamster died.* And a personal favorite: *When people say, "It's a marathon, not a sprint," I don't think they get how much you hate running.*

Living with the low-grade fever of ministry is difficult. And knowing we are called to be Advent people is not the comfort we long for in moments of pain. Being people of promise requires resilience and hope. It's much more desirable to be people of joy and peace rather than longing. However, for each of us who come to Christmastide tired of running a race we didn't sign up for, the good news of Advent is the promise of Emmanuel, God with us.

Today's text is a word of assurance. In Advent we are reminded, and we celebrate that, as Emily McDowell's card proclaims, *This darkness is not a dead end. It's a hallway.* Our identity is rooted in our kinship with God. We belong to God. The words of scripture, offered as context and comfort, remind us that we only know in part (1 Corinthians 13:12), and that gives us the hope and courage we need to carry on.

Advent invites us to honestly name our need and our hope, inviting Christ to be with us in our waiting. Inviting the Holy One to enter into the darkness of our circumstances. In this time, we recognize as a community of faith that things are not all as they should be, that we are in need of a Savior. We celebrate the already of Jesus' birth and honor the not yet of the fullness of God's shalom on earth as it is in heaven. We rest in our belovedness as children of God while awaiting the revelation and clarity that is to come in the second advent.

## BLESSING FOR THE ALREADY AND NOT YET

When you arrive,
    weary and worn—

In the midst
    of a warring world,
    of headlines and sound bites,
    wondering,
    where is the promised light?

In the midst
    of to-do lists and emails,
    family and friends who vie for attention,
    wondering,
    how is this merry and bright?

May you remember it is *already* and *not yet*.

And may you find
    beauty and hope,
    in the tension between
    what is and what will be.

May you claim and proclaim:
    Emmanuel,
    Emmanuel,
    Emmanuel.

*December 3*

# THE DAWN

LECTIONARY READING: ISAIAH 26:16–19

---

O Lord, in distress they sought you;
they poured out a prayer
when your chastening was on them.
Like a woman with child
about to give birth
writhes and cries out in her pain,
so were we because of you, O Lord. **(Isaiah 26:16–17)**

---

Reflecting on the difficulties in the ordinary unfolding of our lives, Anglican priest and author Tish Harrison Warren writes, "Our posture of waiting does not deny the horrors of the night, but it bets on the morning to come."[3] Her honest assertion is the modern-day proclamation of the prophets, for Isaiah knows about waiting. At times, he is crying out to God, pointing out all the problems: *God, you haven't shown up, and look at the mess!*

But Isaiah's pleading implicitly says something else—something rather amazing. The words of Isaiah reveal the ongoing hope. A hope that God will come down and act for the good of all people. And this is the undeniable hope of the Advent season: God has come. God is here. God will come again.

Scripture texts like the passage for today are celebratory, proclaiming the goodness, favor, victory, and restoration that comes from God. They are reminders and invitations to trust in the wisdom, providence, and vision of God's peace.

The movement of the liturgical year carries the people of God through the cycle of the Christian story. We revisit familiar texts, reunite with beloved heroes of faith, and celebrate God's action across time. But it also means that the rhythm of our own journeys or experiences does not always align with the resolution and promised revelation that we honor. Between the providence of hindsight and the compression of the material, we forget that Scripture is a collection of stories from across time, spanning years, centuries, and millennia.

Like the proclaiming prophets, we too are invited to live in those in-between places. In some of our circumstances, we may experience resolution or miraculous intervention. In some places within our lives, we may see God's providence, provision, and redemption. And at times, we find ourselves waiting in the liminal space of not yet.

Advent is the season of waiting. The time when we anticipate the coming of the light. And so, we must acknowledge the reality of darkness—and perhaps even embrace the gifts of night.

Rest and renewal are gifts God gives us through the rhythms of day and night, of fasting and feasting. As we surrender to sleep, we are reminded of our limitations, finitude, and frailty. If we can stay with the discomfort that stirs within us, there are gifts we can receive.

For there, in our own vulnerabilities, God is revealed. Surrendering to our places of lack and acknowledging our needs allow the goodness and grace of God to be manifest. Even more than that, it is in the midst of our vulnerability that God arrives. For God does not take away our vulnerabilities, but through the incarnation, God enters into them.

## BLESSING FOR THE DAWN

On the wild edge,
    on the threshold—
when you are unsure, longing, and vulnerable,
    may you be held with love.

In the distress,
    in the defeat—
when you find that you dwell in the dust,
    may you find the hidden place of peace.

In the long night,
    in the holding vigil—
when you are betting on daylight,
    may you awake to joy.

*December 4*

# ADVENT PEOPLE

LECTIONARY READING: ISAIAH 54:1–8

---

For a brief moment I abandoned you,
but with great compassion I will gather you.
In overflowing wrath for a moment
I hid my face from you,
but with everlasting love I will have compassion on you,
says the LORD, your Redeemer. **(Isaiah 54:7–8)**

---

Although anticipated beginnings may be challenging, the messy middle is often no better. The unresolved tension in the midst of our unfolding story can be as uncomfortable as waiting to start. Threshold spaces can be equal parts stressful and exciting as we face the unknown.

In the days of fresh grief, undergoing cancer treatments, persisting in practices to restore our well-being, or parenting tweens, we long for the after—the gratitude that comes with being through. While we all want to experience the nearness and providence of God, none of us would choose to be in need of a miracle.

Times of great loss can cause us to question everything. This pain can then be amplified when those in our closest community distance themselves from us or deny our questioning in a variety of ways. We feel isolated when we most need companionship. It can feel like the bleak midwinter has entered our souls.

In the field of spiritual formation, stretches of God's silence are referred to as a "dark night of the soul." In these seasons, we recite the promises laid out in Scripture. We look to the saints who have gone before for encouragement. We lean on our community to hold on to hope for us as we long for the promised revelation of God. At times, we may simply cease; we stop engaging in these habits and routines that now feel meaningless.

What does it mean to celebrate Christmas when you no longer have a church home? When you peer into the box holding the nativity set and wonder how you can set out something that represents a story you no longer believe?

The words of familiar carols can feel hollow. *All is well* or *All is calm, all is bright* may feel far from our lived experience. What role do the stories of Scripture play in our lives when we experience more questions than answers?

Advent is a season when we embrace the reality that we see dimly. In Advent, we are reminded that God's time is not our time. The oracle of the Lord that Isaiah proclaims holds together the reality of a soul's midwinter with the promise of what is to come. According to the poetic accounting of the prophet, at times the separation from God we experience is not imagined, unwelcome as it may be (Isaiah 54:7). This is a season for reckoning. How do we live with the griefs of our present circumstances as people who believe in the promise of shalom? Where do we experience God's compassion in the midst of our pain?

These words from the prophet Isaiah are written as a salvation oracle. These poetic proclamations are not an assessment of the current context, but a declaration of hope. These ancient words are an invitation to hearers then and now. A call to patient trust. God's kingdom has always been already and not yet; both and.

In Advent, we long to be comforted. We want to move away from our uncertainty and fear. It's why the traditional themes of peace and joy are heralded in this season. These ideas express what we are deeply craving. We are drawn to these promises because they are a healing balm for the tender and broken pieces of our lives. While we long for comfort and resolution, our faith challenges us, as it does not, usually, offer quick fixes or rescue. Instead, we are invited to embrace patience. We are called to depend on our community. We are asked to trust in the unfolding.

As we follow the thread of God's action throughout time, we recount the stories of God's faithfulness as a claim on what yet could be. Promise is at the heart of the season of Christ's coming. Like the messy middle, it can be an uncomfortable space to stay in. To persist in hope for transformation or relief is vulnerable. Our expectations are both revealing and risky.

## BLESSING FOR ADVENT PEOPLE

In the messy middle,
may you remember
where you have been
and where God has been with you.

In the disorientation and discouragement,
may you remember
you are a recipient of a promise,
and God is faithful.

In the moments of expectation, when you dare to hope,
may you remember
the prophetic words,
and await God's revelation.

*December 5*

# TIMES OF FEAR AND WONDER

LECTIONARY READING: LUKE 1:57–80

---

Fear came over all their neighbors, and all these things were talked about throughout the entire hill country of Judea. All who heard them pondered them and said, "What then will this child become?" For indeed the hand of the Lord was with him. **(Luke 1:65–66)**

---

On the dark mornings of winter, I look forward to my wake-up routine. While it's hard to dig out from the cozy comfort of my bed, once I'm up, I start the wood-burning fireplace in our living room as the coffee perks. With the warm glow and my favorite mug in hand, I proceed with my daily ritual: readings, emails, and a scan through the newspaper. As a child, I thought it was odd that my grandmother started her day by reviewing the obituaries, but I now find it to be a meaningful practice. A pause with gratitude for a new day. A reminder to be about the things that truly matter.

Sometimes I wonder if this is the best way to start my day, as there's no shortage of grief and hardship from droughts and famines, wars and rumors of war, political upheaval and anxiety. On the days that this ritual feels much more devastating than delightful, I tell myself that it is good to be informed; necessary, even. It's tempting to look away, but those of us in the midwinter of a life experience know, there is no turning away. Grief, pain, and disappointment are ever present. Some injustices are so close, some pain points too tender, we cannot look away, even if we wanted to.

The words of the prophets that resound in the Advent texts remind us that the people of God have always borne witness to injustice and pain. God's arrival with justice rolling down and the reign of God's shalom is a promise claimed throughout the ages; a fitting practice to pair with my morning ritual. The soft spaces of our hearts want to turn away from the onslaught of terror and pain. When we are lost, overwhelmed, and grieved, we are tempted to harden our hearts.

We can feel helpless when it seems that the arc of justice is long and very slow in bending toward change. We may take any number of protective measures in the face of disappointment. We may isolate, self-medicate, or try to avoid and deny the reality of the harm we have experienced or the pain we are enduring.

But Scripture entreats us to recite the long-held promises. Zechariah declares: "[God] has shown the mercy promised to our ancestors and has remembered his holy covenant" (Luke 1:72). Scripture calls us to proclaim what is yet to be with hope. "Because of the tender mercy of our God, the dawn from on high will break upon us, to shine upon those who sit in darkness and in the shadow of death, to guide our feet into the way of peace" (Luke 1:78–79).

The words of the prophets remind us of God's vision and promise. So, too, the stories of Scripture tell of the spiritual practice of rightly naming things. In the face of fear, confusion, or wonder, correctly identifying what is happening is part of reflecting the *imago Dei*, the image of God. Just as Adam names the creatures in the creation story (Genesis 2:18–19), we are invited to name the realities of our circumstance, calling out the good and calling for healing and justice in the places of pain.

As Filipina American author Jenai Auman unpacks in her book *Othered*, rightly naming allows us to see things as they truly are.[4] It brings what is hidden to light and reveals assumptions. Rightly naming things forces a reckoning with falsehood.

The practice of rightly naming is one way that we persist in hope, recognizing that things will not always be this way, as we celebrate the double meaning of Advent: Christ has come, Emmanuel, and Christ will come again. We can turn our fear and worry to wonder and hope in the good God will bring forth.

## BLESSING FOR TIMES OF FEAR AND WONDER

In the spaces of unknowing,
    may you be patient,
    choosing wonder and curiosity.

In the spaces of discomfort,
    may you find purpose,
    anticipating change and transformation.

In the spaces of discouragement,
    may you find hope,
    looking for the small shoot of a new thing.

And in the space of the present,
    may you find peace,
    trusting the hand of the Lord is with you.

*December 6*

# DISAPPOINTMENT

LECTIONARY READING: MATTHEW 1:18–20

---

But just when he had resolved to do this, an angel of the Lord appeared to him in a dream and said, "Joseph, son of David, do not be afraid to take Mary as your wife, for the child conceived in her is from the Holy Spirit." **(Matthew 1:20)**

---

While everyone is at church, the dog eats the waiting Christmas ham. Croup, walking pneumonia, or a violent stomach bug comes home with your elementary school student or visiting grandchildren. A slow-going surgery recovery with limitations and complications lingers into the middle of December. A blue Christmas can take many forms.

Inclement weather with howling winds, subzero temperatures, and drifted snow make traveling to the family gathering impossible (or traps you unexpectedly overnight with your extended family!). Christmas Eve is spent in worry and distress at the emergency department of the local hospital. There are many ways to have a disappointing holiday.

A sibling is incarcerated. The death of the family matriarch comes just days before Christmas. A spouse spirals into depression, shutting down as the pace of December events and obligations ratchet up. The circumstances of others can certainly bring stress and change to our traditions, plans, and holiday expectations.

The emphasis on holy waiting and preparation in Advent can seem like a cruel joke when our lives feel chaotic or when we have lost control of our circumstances. Both the invitation to and the focus on anticipation can be like salt in the wound during a holiday season when we must navigate fraught relationships or sit with grief through "the most wonderful time of the year."

In the midst of naming our needs and longings, while we are navigating disappointments, complex circumstances, and challenges, we are reminded to keep watch for the divine presence. Our best efforts, thoughtful solutions, and faithful actions are never lost on God, even if we end up pivoting our plans. Just when Joseph worked out a solution to the unwelcome circumstances he found himself in, a divine invitation (again) changed everything and suggested another way.

The scripture stories of Advent illustrate time and again that when all seems lost, in our longest nights, the divine light shines. In Advent, we hold vigil for a spark of light, the promise of transformation and change. We trust that we are not left alone to figure a way out or through.

Repeatedly, we see disrupted plans and disappointments transformed into miraculous encounters for those who are part of Jesus' birth story: barrenness, unplanned pregnancies, census decrees, angel annunciations, and invitations. The bleakness of midwinter holds the promise of possibility and hope for what will come forth from the work of this season.

Just because the unfolding isn't what we imagined doesn't mean it can't be beautiful. Even though we face unchosen circumstances, it doesn't mean that God can't bring redemption and healing. And so, we continue to stay tender and keep watch for what is yet to come, for what God will do out of the ashes of our expectations and plans.

## BLESSING IN THE MIDST OF DISAPPOINTMENT

May you remember that good news
  is only good news to those in need.

In the midst of grief or disappointment,
  God is with you.
  *Emmanuel.*

May you bear witness to the Advent hope:
  a shoot shall come out of the stump,
  possibility springs forth.

In the midst of pain or loss,
  God is with you.
  *Emmanuel.*

May you bear witness to the Advent promise:
  from what has been cut off,
  from what is broken, discarded, or forgotten,
  new life springs forth.

No matter what you are facing,
  God is with you.
  *Emmanuel.*

*December 7*

# GRIEF

**LECTIONARY READING: 1 SAMUEL 2:1–10**

---

There is no Holy One like the Lord,
no one besides you;
there is no Rock like our God. **(1 Samuel 2:2)**

---

At the midpoint in Advent, word came that my beloved high school history teacher had died. The consequences of a devastating brain tumor he had been diagnosed with at the beginning of summer had rapidly taken their toll. That same week, the grandmother of a church friend passed away unexpectedly. My calendar showed many booked appointments: space for conversation with a friend navigating the first Christmas without her dad, coffee with a colleague marking the first anniversary of her father's death, a phone call with a friend awaiting biopsy results, a long text thread with an out-of-town friend arranging for her parent to move to a nursing home.

For those who have lost loved ones in the holiday season, the pain is often amplified in the upheaval of traditions and expectations. The emphasis on joy and the experience of a grieving heart create painful dissonance. Our journeys with grief are often more complex, extended, and surprising than we anticipate. While we know that loss will visit all of us in many ways throughout our lives, we do not always realize the ways that it will affect us.

It is deeply embedded in our human nature to work to harmonize our lives and our theological beliefs, making sense of our experiences.

We long for a resolution. We look for logical explanations. We rationalize. Sometimes we work to insulate ourselves from future pain. We may deny, ignore, or cover over the depth of our heartache. Navigating the mental gymnastics to establish some sort of equilibrium is exhausting. But masking, pretending everything is okay, is also costly.

And at times, the spaces that should be safest to express our pain are the very places where we experience the greatest incongruity. We hear the refrains of *Joy to the World* and *Gloria in excelsis Deo*. We read familiar scripture passages, prophecies of promise and psalms of praise. When our feelings and current experiences don't resonate, our pain is compounded. We long for the miracles and good news to be real in our wounded places. How can we celebrate when we are still waiting?

The scripture stories were recorded and gathered in times of oppression. They are the record of people who have been on the margins, in need of hope and miraculous, salvific intervention. These texts give us accounts of extraordinary things, yes, but they also record the ways that God cares for the ordinary, the regular folks, by providing for their needs that arise amid the mundane.

The readings for Advent often begin with passages from the prophets; these are proclamations that remind us that throughout time the people of God have been hopeful for change, for revolution. The prophets declared that God's justice would come, and it would arrive through the promised Messiah.

Zechariah's song (Luke 1:68–79) and Mary's Magnificat (Luke 1:46–55) echo Hannah's prayer of rejoicing, our text for today from 1 Samuel 2. These songs proclaim the promise and power of God. All these songs and stories feature women who have known loss, longing, marginalization, and isolation.

The summons of Advent is not to ignore or minimize the dissonance we experience. Instead, we hold our worries and wonderings, our pain and problems, naming the tensions and troubles. And we watch with anticipation for the promised light, the arrival of redemption and renewal.

Our pain does not disqualify us from bearing witness to good news. The complex and imperfect realities of our human existence are the very places that create space for God's presence. And so, we join our voices in song with those who first received the promise and bore witness to the nearness of God.

## BLESSING FOR THE GRIEF

When rather than rejoicing your heart is breaking,
    and the bow of grief releases arrows that strike the heart,
    may you experience the nearness of God.

When you face places of longing, hunger, and barrenness,
    and death and the grave seem near at hand,
    may you experience the nearness of God.

When you find yourself in the ash heap or in the place of darkness,
    and you long for thunder from heaven,
    may you experience the nearness of God;

who comes humbly, vulnerably, and humanly.
Emmanuel.

*December 8*

# WONDER

LECTIONARY READING: LUKE 1:5–17, 24–25

---

In the days of King Herod of Judea, there was a priest named Zechariah, who belonged to the priestly order of Abijah. His wife was descended from the daughters of Aaron, and her name was Elizabeth. Both of them were righteous before God, living blamelessly according to all the commandments and regulations of the Lord. But they had no children because Elizabeth was barren, and both were getting on in years. **(Luke 1:5–7)**

---

Late November brought grey skies and brisk winds. My sister and I drove a few hours over the mountain to attend a weekend retreat. It had been a mad rush to get on the road in time. As much as I needed a break, the preparations it took to be away made me wonder, *Is this really worth it?*

We arrived at the fancy hotel nestled at the base of a dramatic rocky cliff. The line of women waiting to check in was long, and we soon realized there had been a booking error. Would we be willing to accept alternative accommodation? We lugged our bags back to the car and headed across the street. The ramshackle cottage was not what we had in mind, but as the weekend's focus was on gratitude, we felt like we should not complain.

We bundled up and walked back across the road to the meeting room. We were the youngest participants by decades. Increasingly this seemed like a waste of time. And then the speaker began: *Ask someone what they are most grateful for, and they will likely tell you a story about one of the worst experiences of their life.*

While it may initially seem counterintuitive, the pattern holds. It often takes distress or loss to ask for help. Only when we are in desperate need, relieved of our delusions that we are our own sources of good, do we begin to notice God's presence around us.

The truth of this sentiment is evident in the Christmas story. Many of the people who first heralded the good news found themselves in the middle of the worst things that could happen to someone. Zechariah and Elizabeth were blameless yet barren. In their world, being childless was one of the worst things that could happen to them. Yet their grief allowed the angel's announcement and John's miraculous birth to shimmer with even greater brilliance.

For Joseph, to find out the woman he was engaged to was pregnant likely felt like a betrayal, one of the worst things that could happen to him. The person he was going to partner with was now unfit by his cultural standards and expectations. Mary, in saying yes to the divine invitation, forever altered the life she had hoped for herself. She risked her reputation. She risked her future. Likely, she risked her very life.

An unexpected pregnancy, a mandated trip in the late stages of gestation, then a flight to Egypt under threat of death. The characters in the Christmas story are well acquainted with darkness. They experienced fear, disappointment, changes in plans, and an unchosen journey. All these things may have felt, in those moments of great fear and uncertainty, like the worst thing that could happen. In trying to be faithful to God, even with the guidance and assurance of angels, things were still difficult, even fear-inducing at times. There was upheaval and uncertainty. Yet in all this, they were able to participate in the greatest opportunity of their lives.

Advent honors this part of the Christmas account along with the painful parts of our own stories. This threshold season is for you, no matter the form your fear takes. Whether you are awaiting test results, navigating grief, facing broken relationships, or searching for meaning while being on in years, this is a season for you. For it is "from the stump" (Isaiah 11:1) the shoot comes. From what has been discarded and decaying, hope springs forth.

## BLESSING FOR WONDER

In the fog and rain,
  when you wonder
  how to tell the difference between spring and fall . . .

May you remember
  that out from the stump
  a shoot comes.

In the process of transformation,
  when you wonder
  how to differentiate between growing and dying . . .

May you remember
  that brokenness
  is part of beauty.

In all that was and is and is to come,
  when you wonder
  how to distinguish beginning and ending . . .

May you remember
  that the Lord's favor rests
  on those who endure.

*December 9*

# THE SOUL WORK OF ADVENT

LECTIONARY READING: PSALM 71

---

Rescue me, O my God, from the hand of the wicked,
   from the grasp of the unjust and cruel.
For you, O Lord, are my hope,
   my trust, O LORD, from my youth.
From my birth I have leaned upon you,
   my protector since my mother's womb. **(Psalm 71:4–6)**

---

Tears streamed down my face as we navigated the snowy rolling hills on Boxing Day. Our car carried a few containers with the things we would need to make some approximation of home for my mother-in-law at her care facility. We put candles in the windows. The tabletop Christmas tree held just a few of our family's most precious ornaments.

As we hung family photos and covered the hospital bed with a quilt from home, we didn't know that COVID was coming, that we would ultimately say our goodbyes in isolation, gowned and masked. We didn't know that the last visit for our children would be through windowpanes with phones on speaker to say that final *I love you.* While we were grieving that Christmastide, anticipating my mother-in-law's death, we had no idea what was about to unfold. All our ideas, plans, and consolations about how we would make it through evaporated as the global pandemic unfurled.

The gospel accounts of Emmanuel tell the stories of ordinary people who were invited to the extraordinary experience of joining with God in God's work in the world. While we only have small snippets of their lives, we see our own humanity, our own experiences and wonderings reflected in their stories.

We are just like the prophets and priests, shepherds and wise ones, and Mary and Joseph; our honest accounting before God is our greatest act of faith. For when we consent to follow the wind of the Spirit or dare to hope in the face of darkness, we participate in an act of proclamation. We claim the promise of God's faithful intervention. The psalms model how to hold on to hope for redemption and reconciliation without denying our lived experience and our deep need for the kingdom to come on earth as it is in heaven.

While the psalms don't paint the picture of the nativity—there is no shining star, angel host, or band of cloth in a waiting manger—they do honor our experiences. We read and remember the psalms in this season because this collection of sacred poetry is the prayer book of God's people. Within these verses, we find space for all that life holds.

And this is what Advent is for—a time to make ready. Part of that preparation, the soul work of the season, is to bring forward our pains, fears, disappointments, and failings in anticipation of the light that is to come. We are invited to be honest before God about our longings and our needs, the griefs and grievances we carry.

Tensions within families; the deluge of activities, concerts, and events; and the stress of a looming new year—which may bring to mind the perceived failings and disappointments from the year that has passed—all converge in the final weeks of the year. The holidays, we know so well, can be a difficult time.

Advent is not a season for contrived holly jolly, but an invitation to honest reflection. We are invited to connect our lives to God's story and to grasp that thread of hope as we navigate the unfolding.

## BLESSING FOR THE SOUL WORK OF ADVENT

In need of rescue or relief
may you offer praise—
not as one in denial,
but as one who is revealing the deepest truth,
holding need and hope,
on watch for a miracle.

In the face of suffering or injustice
may you offer praise—
not as one naive or helpless,
but as one who is living the deepest truth,
believing that with God
nothing is impossible.

In infirmity or frailty
may you offer praise—
not as one in search of eternity on earth,
but as one who rests in the deepest truth,
trusting in the One
who holds all things.

*December 10*

# THE RECOUNTING

LECTIONARY READING: PSALM 78:1–7

---

Give ear, O my people, to my teaching;
    incline your ears to the words of my mouth.
I will open my mouth in a parable;
    I will utter dark sayings from of old,
things that we have heard and known,
    that our ancestors have told us. **(Psalm 78:1–3)**

---

"It seems the difference between good news and bad news may just be where you are when you receive it," the preacher posited. Consider the prophecies of kings being brought down from their thrones and judgments rendered to those who spent their lives learning and teaching the religious laws and codes. The message of release for the captives and an upside-down kingdom. Position and perspective make all the difference.

Sometimes, holding on to hope feels like foolishness, not blessedness. To continue to believe in things unseen, to hope for what still could be, is a vulnerable posture. Preparing for the worst is somehow more soothing to our nervous systems than staying open to possibility and risking disappointment.

While the Bible contains multitudes—teachings and laws, parables and healing accounts, letters and prophecies—the Psalter is the prayer book of the people of God. The whole range of human emotions is recorded and reflected in these pleas and poems. The psalms help us voice our deepest longings, worries, and fears. They record and retell history. The psalm for today takes a historical view, considering how the past influences the present; it is an attempt to inspire hope and obedience, then and for future generations.[5] It is a plea and a prayer that we would learn the truth of our histories.[6] Whether guarding against disappointment or holding on to hope, the psalms have much to offer us. This liturgy of the people of God can hold our experiences, wonderings, and longings.

We attempt to impose control on our lives, experiences, and circumstances in many different ways (intentionally or otherwise). And we can easily spend so much time and expend so much energy trying to wrangle situations into our control. But the wise ones know this is a fool's errand. Eventually, we all discover how little we actually control.

It's one of the harsh lessons of grief, this lack of control. It's not so much that we have lost control, but that we finally must reckon with our limits. Grief is revealing too. It shows us our expectations, what we had hoped for, what we believed was possible, thought we deserved, or believed to be true.

Writer and practical theologian Kate Bowler writes and talks about how grief is as much about processing the loss of our imagined future as grieving what was lost. In grief, we are not just cut off from the presence of our loved one or their situation but must now reconcile and reimagine what the future will be.

The gospel invitation is to receive good news. And perhaps, at times, this requires that we change our position or perspective. While our histories inform us, our future is still before us, even if it takes shape differently than we had hoped or expected.

We are always bound to the present moment, wrestling with what is, as it is. In Advent, we stand on the threshold, awaiting and anticipating what is yet to be. And we prepare our hearts and minds for what is to come: reimagining our future, holding on to hope for the possibility of transformation, watching for a shoot from the stump, receiving good news.

## BLESSING FOR THE RECOUNTING

The stories we tell will define our lives.
So may you remember:
Bad news is never the final chapter,
for the story is still being told,
there is more to be written.

Just as it was in the beginning,
remember that through God, goodness is given.

The songs we sing will sustain our efforts.
So may you remember:
In the face of darkness and despair,
in the midst of fear and tragedy,
we join our voices together.

Just as the people of God have experienced for generations,
remember that it is part of our calling—
to stand in the space between
the salvation at hand and the salvation yet to be.

The company we keep will carry us on the way.
So may you remember:
We are people of promise,
holding wonder and mystery,
watching and waiting.

Just as Psalms proclaims,
remember that it is God who puts things right.

May it be so.

*December 11*

# COMPOSING A SALVATION ORACLE

LECTIONARY READING: PSALM 85

---

Restore us again, O God of our salvation,
    and put away your indignation toward us.
Will you be angry with us forever?
    Will you prolong your anger to all generations?
Will you not revive us again,
    so that your people may rejoice in you?
Show us your steadfast love, O LORD,
    and grant us your salvation. **(Psalm 85:4–7)**

---

We are all storytellers. The desire to hear, to tell, and to know pulses within each of us. While books are one of my favorite modes of storytelling, humans across time have connected with narrative as a way of making sense of the world. Whether it is a new tale of adventure or familiar words that you can recite from memory, the stories from Scripture, picture books, and movies shape us. Our daily interactions are mostly storytelling experiences, connecting with a friend or loved one through sharing about our lives.

We each remember stories in our own way, and for our own purposes. We all grab on to different facets of the story. As we live into our defining stories—as we tell and retell—we are making meaning of our lives. Sometimes the pieces we remember, or our unique perspectives, open us up to something true and holy. We are shaped by what we choose to highlight, the memories that we carry with us, familiar and well-worn like a worry stone that we might rub smooth in our pocket.

We see this storytelling throughout the Bible, including in poetic form in the Psalms. The scripture text for today is a community lament. And the lament begins with remembering—with telling the story, with putting together memories, assembling pieces of the story. Not only does this remind and encourage us, but it can also give us a new perspective. This practice of giving words to our experiences, needs, and desires is a very powerful, mysterious, and holy act.

The recitation begins with the emphasis not on God's glory but on God's mercy. The greatness recounted draws on God's merciful, faithful love for God's people. While the act of remembering allows us to access hope, it also sets the stage for a call for restoration, a plea for a change in circumstance, a word for what is yet to come. It dares to name and claim the already-and-not-yet reality of God's kingdom, pointing to the vision of shalom that is threaded throughout Scripture. Shaping our own prayers in this way, by focusing on the character and actions of God, moves us from our own fears and limits and connects us to God.

When a psalm follows this format, it is called a salvation oracle. The gathered community of believers has also stood between the salvation at hand and the hope and promise of the salvation yet to be. This psalm of lament and oracle of salvation is ultimately a declaration of hope.

In this threshold season, this time of waiting, the pattern of lament is an appropriate form for our prayers. In our grief and pain, in our heartache and loss, we mirror what the people of God have done for generations. We tell our story, remembering the goodness, recalling where God has been present. And we name our needs before God. We give an honest account of our pain, wonderings, worries, and needs. And then, just as Advent calls us to, we name our hope. We dare to speak of what we long to be true, of what we believe could yet be.

## BLESSING FOR COMPOSING A SALVATION ORACLE

It is both
    the bad news and the good,
    for we are standing at already and not yet
    in so many things.

It is both
    the good news and the bad,
    for Advent is inviting us to trust
    in what yet could be.

It is both
    the bad news and the good,
    for the waiting requires endurance
    in hope of what is to come.

It is both
    the good news and the bad,
    for Christmas is celebrating a promise,
    and in the long stretches of darkness
    that can hardly feel like enough.

*December 12*

# PERSISTENCE

LECTIONARY READING: 1 SAMUEL 1:19–28

---

And she said, "Oh, my lord! As you live, my lord, I am the woman who was standing here in your presence praying to the LORD. For this child I prayed, and the LORD has granted me the petition that I made to him. Therefore I have lent him to the LORD; as long as he lives, he is given to the LORD." **(1 Samuel 1:26–28)**

---

The thread of connection from creation to incarnation, from genesis to revelation, is continued in today's text which highlights the story of "a certain man . . . from the hill country" (1 Samuel 1:1). We learn of the man's beloved wife Hannah, who knows deep longing. What could easily be relegated to details about the birth of the future prophet, priest, and judge Samuel, this account takes on a different significance when it is read as part of the Christmas story.

In her book *Womanist Midrash*, theologian Wilda Gafney reflects on the decision to include Hannah's story in the lectionary selections. Gafney points out that even though Hannah's experience of divine intervention leading to a miraculous pregnancy is not common for women, both in contemporary and ancient times, it is still a powerful story. As Gafney writes, "Her desperation and persistence in prayer transcend time."[7]

Those of us who have wept bitterly and been deeply distressed recognize Hannah's posture. The bargaining and vows offered in hope of fulfillment of our deepest longings is a human disposition. Hannah's faithful, perhaps desperate, petitions—the outpouring of her soul in prayer revealing vexation and anxiety—are relatable feelings for those of us who find ourselves in midwinter seasons of the soul.

This beautiful redemption story, a powerful and miraculous reversal of fortunes, sets up the call and commission of Samuel. Its themes echo through the stories of the women connected to the nativity. Yet these Advent stories can be difficult to hear each year when our own longing and need persists. Where is our miracle? Where is God's provision, love, and care? Do our prayers and petitions make a difference?

"In her vowing and praying, Hannah crafts an innovation that would change Israelite religion," writes Gafney. "She prays privately, believing that God can and will hear the prayers of her heart. This is revolutionary! The practice of the time was to pray aloud, to ensure God could hear the petitioner."[8]

While Hannah experiences a miracle, her story is so much more. Yes, she births a child who will become a hero in the faith tradition. But her contributions are not limited to her reproductive ability. In Hannah's story, we learn from and lean on her persistence and posture in prayer. We learn from her bold and wild hope in what may yet be possible even as she offers it in desperation. Her pain and longing was recognized and acknowledged by those around her. And then she receives a word of blessing.

But what does it mean to go in peace when the ache remains? Others' words of blessing can ring hollow when longing persists. Perhaps the Advent invitation within this text is to connect with the revelation of God through Hannah, whose life illustrates, like Elizabeth and Mary, God's ability to create life amid seeming impossibility.

While our own specific experiences may not embody the gift of new life through a longed-for child, these examples stand out as reminders that our God is always about bringing shalom, reconciliation, and fulfillment. Though God's response to our supplications may be unexpected or detached from our preferred timelines, it is always one of connection and presence.

## BLESSING FOR PERSISTENCE

When your rivals provoke and irritate,
when your heart is sad,
when you have presented yourself before God,
may you be loved.

When you are distressed,
when you are weeping,
when you are bitter,
may you be seen.

When you make vows,
when you bargain,
when you continue to pray,
may you be blessed.

*December 13*

# THE BARREN SPACES

LECTIONARY READING: JUDGES 13:2–7

---

There was a certain man of Zorah, of the tribe of the Danites, whose name was Manoah. His wife was barren, having borne no children. And the angel of the Lord appeared to the woman and said to her, "Although you are barren, having borne no children, you shall conceive and bear a son." **(Judges 13:2–3)**

---

Ahead of our extended family gathering one year, I sent an email. Carefully crafting words, deleting and starting again (and again), I named the pain of our journey with infertility. *At this point in time, inquiries about pregnancy are more harmful than helpful. We look forward to being together and prefer to talk about other things.* The tenderness of uncertainty and the grief of this unchosen journey felt too fraught to engage.

Attending church and singing carols was challenging too. Pregnancy, birth, and babies are such a focus of the Christmas season. When your arms are empty, the elevation of these images and motifs can feel particularly grievous. While the incarnation is a new thing, the way God announces the plan, the way that things unfold, is in line with tradition and Hebrew Scripture's prototypes—angel messengers and acts of God that open wombs.

The Advent texts don't just give us the story of Mary, Joseph, and the birth of Jesus, but also a parallel story of Elizabeth and Zechariah. And those names should call to mind the stories of Abraham and Sarah, who birthed Isaac: all the nations of the earth shall be blessed. Elkanah and Hannah, who had Samuel: for this child I prayed. Manoah and his wife, who bore Samson: a man of God came to me (see Genesis 18; 1 Samuel 1; Judges 13).

In the Hebrew Scriptures, barrenness signals more than infertility. Within the patriarchal culture of the day, barrenness was a commentary on a woman's failure, a kind of code for worthlessness, an occasion for sorrow and shame. But this intended curse becomes the birthplace of an unexpected blessing, an opportunity for the unbelievable, the miraculous. God is telling a different story. While Scripture records this plight of fear and affliction, it implicitly invites us into connection, it offers us an opportunity to find ourselves in the story of God's goodness and grace. Perhaps more than any specific experience of childbearing or infertility, barrenness illustrates the way that each of us has had to wrestle with feelings of inadequacy. We have all questioned our worth and worthiness.

The story of Elizabeth and Zechariah's waiting is not just a story for women or for those among us who struggle with infertility. For all of us who face unchosen journeys, for those of us who know longing, this is a story for all who are wanting and waiting. In fact, it's a perennial question: *If I cannot produce, will I still be loved and accepted?* The pressure and temptation to prove our worth continue to echo in our current contexts.

Our own barren spaces are uncovered when we experience loss, when we question our value, or when our imagined future slips away. Perhaps you've lost a job that gave you meaning and supported your family, or you've lost respect or esteem through events not of your own doing. Maybe you were denied a promotion or were betrayed by a loved one. Loss also comes through the natural course of aging: physical limitations, terminal diagnosis, chronic conditions. And we wonder, *Does my life matter?*

In these scriptural accounts, the context of barrenness should alert us to a miracle in whatever follows. For in each of these stories, longing was an invitation to prayer, to conversation with the divine. Most of us have been in that space. We have all encountered a situation where we were desperate for God's intervention, having come to the end of what we could achieve or make happen.

Perhaps the places of barrenness in your life are opportunities for God's revelation. Perhaps this Advent you join with the line of women, Sarah and Hannah, Elizabeth and Mary, who bear God's promise and unexpected joy.

## BLESSING FOR THE BARREN SPACES

When you examine your unfulfilled longings,
the seemingly empty spaces,
may you nourish the tender and tenacious hope of promise
and unexpected joy.

When you are *getting on in years* and it seems too late now,
may the places of longing bear witness to miracles.

When it seems that scars and gaps are telling the story,
may you join with Elizabeth in naming,
*this is what the Lord has done for me.*

When you wonder if it even ever mattered, *how can it be?*
may the open spaces of your life be the container for the Spirit.

And in so doing,
may your barren spaces become places of blessing.

*December 14*

# UNIMAGINED POSSIBILITIES

LECTIONARY READING: LUKE 1:26–38

---

But she was much perplexed by his words and pondered what sort of greeting this might be. **(Luke 1:29)**

---

Holding space for people as their lives fall apart is a sacred and scary task. Bearing witness to the pain of the unraveling, of infidelity and betrayal, or of grief requires a particular resilience, as this is not something a companion can fix, control, or help.

In one particularly complex situation, I recall my own negative internal response when a counselor suggested someone in my congregation should adopt a posture of radical acceptance. The therapist explained that acknowledging difficult or painful realities could be a path toward healing. When I heard this, I was unsettled. My sense of justice cried out. How could surrender be the path toward peace?

The truism behind the counselor's invitation is that acceptance doesn't equal approval. We don't have to appreciate our circumstances to embrace the reality that is before us. However, until we engage in the truth of what we are facing, we are stuck. Radical acceptance empowers us to make decisions and move on.

Time revealed that the decision to embrace this counsel was a significant turning point for my congregant. While the ultimate resolution of circumstance was not what they would have preferred or envisioned, accepting reality opened up new, life-giving possibilities. Letting go of the pains of the past and a particular imagined future recovered and redirected energy, sparking a new kind of hope.

The stories of annunciation illustrate this radical acceptance, which closely parallels the spiritual discipline of "practicing the present." As a sacred habit, practicing the present invites us to tend to what is happening in the moment. Our minds are often so focused on the future or stuck in resentments about past harms that we miss the gifts and opportunities of the present moment. A practice of the present brings awareness to what is and it opens minds and hearts to spiritual growth, connection with God, and sacred possibility.

Like Mary and Elizabeth, we have the opportunity to respond to God's invitation. Sure, the request may not be what we had imagined for our lives. The timing may feel all wrong. We may doubt our abilities, our sense of the Spirit, or the consequence of embarking on such a mission. When we receive our own invitation, the questions may come. What will this mean? Why me?

An angel's appearance. A proclamation. God's presence and assurance amid an ordinary day and an unbelievable invitation. The record of encounters with divine conversation partners. When we meet God in our own lives, wonder is an appropriate response. *What kind of greeting is this? How can this be?*

The stories of annunciation invite us to consider how we respond to divine encounters and invitations of the Spirit. At times, the best way forward may be to relinquish the fight against reality. Embracing what is happening allows us to turn our energies toward other questions and actions. Are we receptive to the work of God in our lives, even in circumstances that we wouldn't choose for ourselves? What has it been like to ponder the cost and consequences of saying yes to God's invitation?

Sometimes our response to God is wonder, amazement, or concern. Sometimes our response to a divine conversation may be a quiet reflection. And sometimes, our response to God's invitation to participate in the kingdom work is *yes, let it be with me.*

## BLESSING FOR UNIMAGINED POSSIBILITIES

When the angel arrives . . .
  a flutter
  a knowing nudge

And you wonder
  *what kind of greeting this might be*?

When the opportunity comes . . .
  an invitation
  a question

And you wonder, much perplexed,
  *how can this be?*

When nothing is impossible with God
  a hope
  a challenge—

There is work to be done.
*Let it be with me.*

*December 15*

# COMMUNITY

LECTIONARY READING: LUKE 1:39–45

In those days Mary set out and went with haste to a Judean town in the hill country, where she entered the house of Zechariah and greeted Elizabeth. When Elizabeth heard Mary's greeting, the child leaped in her womb. And Elizabeth was filled with the Holy Spirit and exclaimed with a loud cry, "Blessed are you among women, and blessed is the fruit of your womb." **(Luke 1:39–42)**

A few years ago, the US Surgeon General raised the alarm of a pending loneliness epidemic. The symptoms of anxiety, depression, and other physical illnesses can be exacerbated in those who are alone. Technology affords us opportunities and options that belie the artifice and gaps that many of us live with. Even before the global coronavirus pandemic led to forced isolation and forever altered the way people gather and interact, the impacts of loneliness were cracking the foundations of contemporary culture and community.

Loneliness comes in many forms. It's not just for those who are single or widowed. Many people are lonely even when surrounded by a community. Spouses are stuck in loveless marriages, parents are estranged from children, children are ostracized by family, and friends cut their ties over a long forgotten argument or perhaps over a wound that will not heal. The statistics are startling. The implications are significant. And the holiday season only amplifies these tensions and losses. Expectations and traditions can amplify the grief and pain of separation and desolation.

It's unfortunate that the church is often the place where people feel most alone and that the holy celebration of Jesus' birth can be a difficult time for many. For God has always been calling and collecting people. God's design for humanity has always been to be within community. God's mission and work in the world has always been drawing people together through reconciling relationships, as the scripture stories illustrate again and again.

It is no surprise that Mary goes to be with Elizabeth upon accepting the divine invitation. These women share an experience and connection, though the realities of God's call had different implications. The community and support these kinfolk find in each other insulates and encourages them as they navigate the beauty and challenge of saying yes to God.

The practice of community not only reflects God's call and command but also helps us to reflect the image of God more fully. We need each other. The fruit of our lives is nurtured and enriched by everything we learn when we are with people, by sharing the journey of life, the joys and the hardships.

Of course, putting ourselves in proximity can be more discipline than practice. People are thoughtless, sometimes even cruel. We misunderstand one another and wound each other through our assumptions, ignorance, and differences. Relationships are hard work. They often require more than we believe we can give, both in time and resources. It requires humility, forgiveness, vulnerability, and patience. But we cannot love people generally. Our faith must have specificity.

Women at the margins were the first to receive the promise of Advent. This theme echoes throughout the Gospels, including after Jesus' crucifixion when another Mary is the first to witness, both to see and to proclaim, the good news of Jesus' resurrection. It was to those who weren't valued in society that God first revealed Godself. It was to those on the margins that good news was entrusted, discovered, and proclaimed.

The invitation, promise, and intervention of God continues to come to those of us who find ourselves on the margins this Advent. Isolated and alone, whether physically or spiritually, it is for those such as us that the good news comes.

## BLESSING FOR COMMUNITY

In calling and commission
    may you make haste,
    finding companions for the journey.

In wonder and fear
    may you welcome others,
    sharing in all that the journey holds.

In joy and delight
    may you experience blessing,
    celebrating the journey with others.

*December 16*

# THE DIVINE INVITATION

LECTIONARY READING: LUKE 1:46–56

---

And Mary said,
"My soul magnifies the Lord,
and my spirit rejoices in God my Savior,
for he has looked with favor on the lowly state of his servant.
**(Luke 1:46–48)**

---

"All the girls wanted to be Mary," my son told me as he recounted the casting process for the upcoming nativity play. His pageant excitement sparked my own imagination. Perhaps for seven-year-old girls, being Mary was appealing. But as a middle-aged mother, I felt the questions and complexities arise. My most haunting consideration was on the words of Simeon at the time of Jesus' temple dedication when he was just a few days old. Simeon ominously told Mary, "A sword will pierce your own soul, too" (Luke 2:34–35).

Of course, by then it's too late. Mary has already said yes; she's birthed the baby. She's all in, like it or not. Would it have been different if the angel Gabriel had included this detail in the annunciation?

Every time angels show up, they offer the admonition "Fear not!"—indicating that an angel's appearance and invitation may not be so much comforting and exciting as shocking and terrifying. Perhaps that's why Mary rushed to be with Elizabeth. She longed for the comfort of one who knew longing and uncertainty. Their shared experiences brought them comfort and courage in the midst of something extraordinary and unbelievable.

When God's call is revealed in our lives, it is often overwhelming because God asks things of us we cannot do on our own; God invites us to be challenged, to be vulnerable, to be reliant on the Spirit's guidance. When God invites us to participate in the work of God's kingdom, it requires giving what we are, who we are, our very selves. Just like Mary. She gives her body and offers her reputation. Her yes changed the trajectory of everything.

When we submit to God's invitation in our lives, our own souls are pierced. To live out our faith means to know and love God's created ones. It requires suffering with others. We cannot share good news and be unaffected by the realities of a broken world. In those moments, a prophetic vision can feel like powerlessness. Like Mary at the annunciation, we wonder, *How can this be?*

Our culture says that pain and discomfort are to be avoided at all costs. But the stories of our faith tradition remind us that grief and joy, lament and rejoicing, and excitement and terror are all part of what it means to be a disciple of Christ.

Our honest conversation with God is our greatest act of faith, for in that act we claim the promise of God's faithful intervention, holding on to hope for redemption and reconciliation without denying the lived experience and the deep need for the kingdom to come on earth as it is in heaven. And so, we know that Advent is for us, the ones who know suffering, whose souls have been pierced while responding to God's invitation through loving others and through opening ourselves to hope once more.

## BLESSING FOR THE INVITATION

When the Word arrives: *Fear not!*
and you are surprised, afraid
may you be open to a yes.

When you assent: *Let it be with me.*
and then you wonder, worry
may you find a companion with shared experience.

When the prophetic word is spoken:
*A sword shall pierce your own soul, too.*
and you are overwhelmed and broken open
may you experience the nearness of the Holy One.

*December 17*

# BEING HUMAN

LECTIONARY READING: PSALM 68:4–13

---

Sing to God; sing praises to his name;
    lift up a song to him who rides upon the clouds—
his name is the Lord—
    be exultant before him.
Father of orphans and protector of widows
    is God in his holy habitation. **(Psalm 68:4–5)**

---

The poetry and promise of the Psalms give voice to our experiences. Praise and lament, vexation and vindication are all held in the songbook of God's people. The psalms are more than a collected work of art or liturgy for worship; they are prayers that form and inform us. As we engage with the problems and promises they reflect, we are changed. Our perspectives change; our hope is renewed. "The transformation they effect isn't to turn our sadness into happiness," writes Anglican priest Tish Harrison Warren. The psalms "fix our vision on God's love for us and teach us to locate our own pain and longing in God's eternal drama. They form us into a people who can hold the depths of our sorrow with utter honesty even as we hold to the promises of God."[9]

Today's text is a psalm that proclaims God's reign. It is a liturgy of dependence on the power of God.[10] The themes and songs of the Christmas story echo the psalmist's refrains. Mary and Zechariah declare, "My soul magnifies the Lord" and "Blessed be the God of Israel." They speak of how God has "lifted up the lowly, . . . saved [us] from the hand of all who hate us, . . . rescued [us] from the hands of our enemies," and "come to the aid of his child" (see Luke 1:46–55 and 1:68–79). Their powerful songs, the Magnificat and the prophecy of Zechariah, echo the truth and theology of the Psalms, demonstrating that God has always taken an interest in the well-being of the lowly. Our God is a compassionate deity concerned with those who need help.

At times we may experience our vulnerability as a failure, but our faith teaches that our vulnerability is precisely what allows us to access the power of God. Scripture reminds us that those who are blessed are the poor in spirit, the mourning, the meek, the merciful, and the peacemakers (Matthew 5:3–11).

Advent invites us to pull off the mask of pretending. It is a sacred and protected space to name the reality of our experiences, to reveal the longing in our lives, the imperfection, and our need for God's mysterious and miraculous intervention. We tell our secrets to God, and in so doing, our prayers and petitions in this time join with the strains of God's people throughout time. Lament or praise, historical or prophetic, psalms are a recorded dialogue between God and God's people. As scholar Willem VanGemeren highlights, "The beauty of hope in the Psalter lies in keeping the tension between the present world and the anticipated enjoyment of new creation."[11]

During Advent, we boldly name the tension of already and not yet. We proclaim the goodness and grace we have received and name our ongoing need. The psalm for today remembers God's action: "When you went out before your people, when you marched through the wilderness . . . in your goodness, O God, you provided for the needy" (Psalm 68:7, 10). The text pleads for continued grace and action: "Summon your might, O God; show your strength, O God, as you have done for us before" (v. 28).

We bear our scars and present our wounds while heralding the hope of what is to come. The psalms, writes Kathleen Norris, "defeat our tendency to try to be holy without being human first."[12] Christmastide celebrates this human and holy reality of incarnation that changes everything.

## BLESSING FOR BEING HUMAN

*Let God rise up!*

In your loneliness and grief and
in your isolation and loss,
may you find rest in the holy habitation.

*Let God rise up!*

In your captivity and bondage and
in your drought and discouragement,
may you dwell in God's goodness.

*Let God rise up!*

In your weakness and vulnerabilities and
in your fears and failings,
may you encounter the grace of God.

*Let God rise up!*

*December 18*

# OUR EXPECTATIONS

LECTIONARY READING: ISAIAH 66:10–13

---

As a mother comforts her child,
so I will comfort you;
you shall be comforted in Jerusalem. **(Isaiah 66:13)**

---

"I'm going to describe something, and I want you to guess what it is," the pastor said as she began the children's message. She gave a few clues: "It lives in trees, and it eats nuts." Strangely, no hands went up. The pastor moved on to physical descriptors: "It is furry and sometimes brown or grey." The tension in the room was rising, whispers and rustles as people shifted in their pews. "It has a long bushy tail . . ."

Finally, one little boy tentatively raised his hand. The pastor breathed a sigh of relief and called on him. "Well . . . ," said the boy, "I know the answer is Jesus, but it sounds like you're talking about a squirrel!"

One of the human challenges made evident in Advent is that of right expectation. Sometimes we are so formed by certainty, preoccupied with how things have been in the past, or so set on a particular iteration of the future, that we miss out on what God has done, is inviting us to do, or is already doing. Certainly, Advent and Christmas are about Jesus. But sometimes we miss something in the message or the connection to our present experience because we believe we know the answer, or we've been taught there is only one appropriate interpretation or response.

Concluding the book of Isaiah, today's scripture passage returns to the themes of comfort and hope in poetic prophecy. The images of labor and birth evoke hope, announcing and confirming God's design and ability to do the unexpected, inviting us to trust in what is yet to come. Pregnancy and parenthood are apt illustrations of upended expectations and the intertwining of great fear and great joy.

You don't have to have experienced the swell of a belly or sleepless nights of newborn care to identify with Isaiah's text. The Christmas story is threaded through with encounters of the unexpected, foreshadowing Jesus' life and ministry (as so many in his company missed or misunderstood because the way of Jesus defied their expectations). We can all relate to being surprised, or at times devastated, when situations and circumstances don't match our predictions and assumptions.

At times, the grief we experience in our lives is due to our own misplaced expectations. When people inevitably miss the mark, when things don't unfold as we had counted on, when we don't reach our goals, or when things don't go according to plan, the dissonance between what is and what we had hoped for is distressing. But a beautiful, faithful life doesn't mean an experience without pain or hardship. The work of discipleship is that of continual remaking and ongoing transformation.

As much as Advent is a beginning, it also honors the messy middle of our experiences. This stretch of weeks honors the "between" times, the liminal spaces in our lives. The soul work of Advent is to expand our trust, alertness, and awareness of God so that we can receive the gifts of wonder, delight, and transformation. We may do well to consider what expectations we are holding for this time. What might we release or reconsider in this season?

## BLESSING FOR OUR EXPECTATIONS

When the longings, laments, and barren spaces of your life loom large
may you consider the gifts of emptiness, spaciousness, and need
that make room
to receive the way and wonder of our faithful and miracle-
working God.

When the assumptions, hopes, and dreams you have imagined for
yourself are dashed
may you consider the gifts of hibernation, gestation, and all that
happens below the surface
in the quiet, dark, hidden spaces of the natural world.

When the prospects, possibilities, and promises you have long awaited
turn to dust
may you consider the ache and agony of birthing a new thing
trusting in the movement, transformation, and emergence of
new life.

*December 19*

# THE ASH HEAP

LECTIONARY READING: PSALM 113

---

He raises the poor from the dust
and lifts the needy from the ash heap. **(Psalm 113:7)**

---

At times, words escape us. Perhaps a song stirs something within us, connecting us to a deeper experience or expression of our pain or hope. When we do not know what to say, we can turn to the words of Scripture and the prayers of God's people that have endured for generations to bring expression to our longing.

In the songbook of God's people, communal prayers and poems shape the liturgy. This particular psalm of praise is a reminder of God's power. The images of this psalm—the ash heap and the barrenness—call to mind our distressing situations, the circumstances in which we feel abandoned, or our moments of despair where we are unable to bring change or transformation by way of our own will and abilities. God is the one who creates the new reality, even when it seems impossible.

Of all the psalms, today's passage draws most closely from the themes and phrases in Hannah's song of praise (1 Samuel 2:1–10). These ideas are also echoed in the story of Elizabeth's pregnancy and Mary's Magnificat (Luke 1:46–55). These words of promise and acclaim are lifted up not to cover over the disappointment, pains, and griefs of our experience but as a reminder that out of the desolation and destruction, God's good news and salvific action emerge.

The stories and psalms of the Advent season are not counterpoints to our grief. Instead, this powerful, confident, and declarative poetry reminds us what a prayer of hope may look like. It shows us how we are connected to the bigger story arc of God's people across time and in many places. In proclaiming hope, Psalms reminds us that redemption is also an Advent longing.

For those of us who are suffering, redemption is a beautiful hope. Redemption is not merely a resolution, but a recognition that there is no going back, no return to the before. After we have experienced heartbreak, nothing can replace what was. Nor is this a season of silver-lining pain, calling on some heavenly hope that denies earthly realities or attempts to wrestle the loose ends of loss into a tidy bow. Contending with the growing dark of our experiences and offering raw honesty is what the season of Advent is for.

Redemption promises a reckoning, an acknowledgment of the pain, and an accounting of the losses. "Redemption," writes Tish Harrison Warren, "does not skip over the darkness, but demands that every last tear run."[13] It reminds us that God will meet us at the ash heap and in our barrenness. Divine encounters await us in the places that we are most anxious to escape or avoid. As Warren writes, "To trust God in our vulnerability is to willingly enter a lifelong exercise in becoming attuned to what blessing truly is and how it is often found in the last place we'd look for it."[14]

When we acknowledge our limits and longings, when we become "intimate with our fragility and finitude," we are able to connect with God in a new and deeper way.[15] When we persist in prayer amid chaos and pain, we access a power greater than our own as an anchor against the swirl of hopelessness. And as Warren reminds us, in Christmas we recognize and celebrate that somehow, "mysteriously, God does not take away our vulnerability."[16] Instead, God enters into it. God joins with us.

## BLESSING FOR THE ASH HEAP

May you find words
in the witness
of those who have gone on before.

May you find confidence
in the vision of shalom.

May you find courage
in the stories
of those from then and now.

May you find peace
in the promise of shalom.

May you find hope
in the sacred thread
of faith that trusts in what is
to come.

*December 20*

# THE LONG TIMES

LECTIONARY READING: MATTHEW 1:20–25

---

An angel of the Lord appeared to him in a dream and said, "Joseph, son of David, do not be afraid to take Mary as your wife, for the child conceived in her is from the Holy Spirit. She will bear a son, and you are to name him Jesus, for he will save his people from their sins." **(Matthew 1:20–21)**

---

Today's scripture passage sums up nearly a year in five short verses, masking the angst and ache that often comes with anticipation and waiting. Ask nearly any pregnant woman in her third trimester and she will attest to the long wait of forty weeks of gestation. Pregnancy and birth are painful, messy, and all-consuming as much as beautiful, holy, and miraculous.

The number forty features significantly throughout Scripture. Noah and his family endured forty days and nights of rain in the story of the great flood. Moses spent forty days on the mountain with God. The people of God spent forty years wandering in the wilderness. After Jesus' baptism, he spent forty days in fasting and prayer in the desert. Whether literal or metaphorical, forty days or forty years signifies a long time. Is it coincidence or poetic justice that pregnancy, too, lasts forty weeks?

Theology professor Wendy Wright found new meaning in the Advent season after her own experience of pregnancy. When one is pregnant, she notes, there is no break from being with child. For the time, it is a perpetual state of being. There is no holiday from the demands that pregnancy makes of your body. It impacts how you engage in everything you do.[17] In this way, pregnancy can be a rich metaphor for the spiritual experience. Wonderful and worrisome, exciting and exasperating all at once, so too our discipleship journey is all-encompassing. The commitment to follow in the way of Jesus affects every part of our lives.

We see this pattern throughout Scripture, and we bear witness to this reality in our own lives. Faith in God through Jesus is always a deeply personal and individual commitment. Yet mysteriously, it is also always communal, the impacts reaching beyond me and my own life. Divine revelation and divine encounters require more than we believed they would, pushing us beyond what we imagined. It changes our plans and ideas. Like Joseph, we may receive a divine invitation that upends our expectations and rewrites our dreams.

Following Jesus will change everything about our lives. It's a complete reorientation. But perhaps the surprise is that we continue to experience reorientation and transformation even after our initial faith commitment. Too often we look to religion to provide comfort, solutions, and answers to all our questions. And in Advent, we remember that God offers us companionship. The divine joins us in our humanity and accompanies us through suffering, waiting, uncertainty, and ongoing change.

The miracle of Christmas and the truth of the angelic message took time to be revealed. As artist Scott Erickson reflects, incarnation is all about the journey of the hidden becoming seen, and the cost of this kind of revelation is that it always changes everything.[18]

The healing, redemption, and restoration that comes in God's shalom isn't a return to what was. Pregnancy and birth leave their indelible marks. Our past losses and griefs still have an impact. Advent rightly names the brokenness and shadow in our lives. It compels us to hold on to the resurrection hope that we find in God through Christ, the promise of transformation and wholeness. The beauty and gift of Christmas is that "the incarnation always brings good news, but it never minimizes the realness of our pain."[19]

## BLESSING FOR THE LONG TIMES

In the crucible of waiting
may you find manna—a sign.

In the darkness of the long night
may you find a glimmer of light—a spark.

In the pain of unmet longing
may you find hope—a reorientation.

In the wonder of *what now?*
may you find comfort—a companion.

In the weeks of Advent
may you find good news—a savior.

*December 21*

# MIDWIFERY

## LECTIONARY READING: LUKE 2:1–7

---

> While they were there, the time came for her to deliver her child. And she gave birth to her firstborn son and wrapped him in bands of cloth and laid him in a manger, because there was no place in the guest room. **(Luke 2:6–7)**

---

When I served on a pastoral team, our division of responsibilities meant that I only preached a few times a year, and only on designated texts and themes to fit into our planned preaching series. Therefore the first sermon I preached was on the theme of judgment. As I lamented this unfortunate assignment with my senior pastor, he sagely said, "The problem you are recognizing is that people come to church to be comforted, not challenged."

In embracing a call to ministry and training at seminary, I was eager and inspired to form people and to break open the Word of God. I was taught and believed that as a pastor, I was called and commissioned to disciple people and strengthen their faith. But in the reality of practice, I discovered people want to be comforted, not challenged. It's probably why the pews are often fullest on the holy days of Christmas and Easter. The gathering and rituals of worship are part of our family traditions and celebrations; we sing the beloved carols and hear familiar stories that reassure us and put us at ease.

But the problem is that a comfortable faith isn't much good when trouble comes your way; "#blessed" and "everything happens for a reason" don't stand up to the experience of life in this world. We need a robust faith. The *I have wrestled with an angel and now walk with a limp* faith. A faith that can hold questions and embrace mystery. A faith that sits in silence with a grieving friend, that *does for the least of these* (see Genesis 32:22–31; Matthew 25:40).

In the same season that I was writing that first sermon, I came across an interview with academic Brené Brown where she reflected on the role of faith over the course of her life. She described an epiphany moment when she realized that faith is to function as a midwife, not an epidural.

It was an evocative way to name the disconnect that I was experiencing as I began pastoral ministry. So many of us are taught that belief in God will protect us from hardship and pain, and that doing the right things will lead to a life of ease and blessing. We expect inoculation from grief, an epidural for life. But what the community of faith has to offer, what the gift of the incarnation offers, is companionship, a midwife as we navigate the labor pains of bringing life into this world.

As we near the celebration of Christmas and the heralded refrains of peace, love, hope, and joy resound, we remember that the invitation of Advent is to receive these gifts in proper context: embraced in the midst of pain as a balm for our wounds.

These familiar, yet theologically rich, words don't represent a conditional attitude or reality but are instead a fruit of faith. Christian hope doesn't deny the existence of suffering and pain. Instead, it embraces God's power to heal, mend, and restore. Christian love doesn't dull the ache; it companions us through whatever unfolds. Christian peace does not simply pacify conflict, but it moves us toward reconciliation. Christian joy doesn't ignore loss and grief but amplifies the connections we do have. May we receive the gifts of peace, love, hope, and joy in these days.

## BLESSING FOR MIDWIFERY

In the longing for comfort
may the gift of challenge
strengthen you.

In the longing for relief
may the gift of endurance
assist you.

In the longing for resolution
may the gift of hope
companion you.

And may you find
the gift of God's presence
through Spirit, friend, and sacred stranger
is enough
to navigate today.

*December 22*

# THE (EXTRA)ORDINARY

LECTIONARY READING: LUKE 2:8–14

---

Now in that same region there were shepherds living in the fields, keeping watch over their flock by night. Then an angel of the Lord stood before them, and the glory of the Lord shone around them, and they were terrified. **(Luke 2:8–9)**

---

During a routine night on the job, God showed up in a spectacular way. The shepherds were doing their ordinary work, lowly work by all accounts. In the middle of the ordinary, they encountered the extraordinary. Somehow, their moment of great fear was an invitation and opportunity to receive great joy.

So, too, our most ordinary moments may lead to encounters with God. Perhaps that may be when it is most likely! When, in the course of doing life, something interrupts our routines or subverts our expectations, when we face something that startles or disturbs us, the moment of fear or terror may be the very threshold that can bridge into great joy.

It was an ordinary night watching over their flocks when opportunity knocked, an unexpected invitation arrived. When the angelic host showed up, amid great fear, the shepherds had to make a choice. Would they let fear hinder them? These were just ordinary people going about their work. People who had worries and needs, to-do lists, and responsibilities. People who were in need of a Savior but also resigned to the reality of their circumstances. Perhaps they were people trying to hold on to hope but felt rather hopeless.

The routines of our lives can grow mundane. We can become bored by the ordinary and long for something spectacular. At other times, the ordinary can overwhelm us. In the routine tasks and many demands, we wonder where is joy and peace? Is there any hope for a turning or change?

For many, the scripture texts that recount the Christmas story are familiar. With so much distance from the original context, it is easy to lose the gravity and meaning of these words. To those first hearers, good news meant something specific. Good news was a proclamation and broad announcement of great import. For those in the first century, good news was connected to the empire. It was used to connote an emperor's birth or a military conquest.

Luke is telling us something significant. The nativity is not just a religious happening. This amazing fulfillment of a long-awaited prophecy is also a turning point in history—a threshold moment of something new and amazing that God is doing.

When we hear "threshold moment," we may think that the beginning is obvious. But it is not always so. Sometimes it takes distance or hindsight to recognize that a new chapter has already begun. Sometimes it takes thoughtful reflection, remembering—that is, putting the pieces back together—to notice the ways that God was present, that the light was dawning, and that something new was taking shape.

The good news often arrives in our lives in surprising and unexpected ways. It can upend our ordinary routines and habits. And the good news will affect everything about our lives. It always has wholehearted implications. The whole of our lives is affected by our commitment to the way of Jesus.

On the precipice that is Advent, the good news and great joy that the shepherds received centuries ago is still good news. In this season we acknowledge that the reconciling work of God continues. Like the shepherds, we are given the opportunity to respond to God's presence and work as it arrives in the middle of ordinary things. It will surprise, perhaps frighten us. It will invite us into risk and wonder. And if we are alert and responsive, we can participate in a miraculous revelation.

## BLESSING FOR THE (EXTRA)ORDINARY

May you simply be.
Be you.
Be faithful in the ordinary, the mundane, the everyday.

May you simply wait.
Notice.
Be present to what is, right now, in this moment.

And when the invitation comes,
  when the sky breaks forth with light,
  in the moments of fear,
  when good news comes near . . .

May you simply go.
Believe.
Be one who experiences the extraordinary.

*December 23*

# WAITING

LECTIONARY READING: LUKE 2:15–20

---

So they went with haste and found Mary and Joseph and the child lying in the manger. When they saw this, they made known what had been told them about this child, and all who heard it were amazed at what the shepherds told them, and Mary treasured all these words and pondered them in her heart. The shepherds returned, glorifying and praising God for all they had heard and seen, just as it had been told them. **(Luke 2:16–20)**

---

It will not always be like this, for nothing stays the same. We easily get trapped in ruminating on the past, the "if only." Or we can become obsessed with what could be when we get through this. But the truth is that we can only effect change in the present moment. We cannot change the past, and really, we cannot do something in the future. We can only be in the present.

Accepting the reality of our current situation does not equate to approving of the present circumstances. However, acknowledging the facts of our current season helps us get our bearings. It reorients us. It offers us a way forward because healing requires honesty. It requires releasing what we thought would be or what we believe should be to embrace what is happening.

Growth requires letting go. Nature illustrates this in the change of the seasons. Through the aging process, we are reminded that our bodies change too. This practice of release is threaded throughout our lives—we just don't always notice the ways we have experienced it.

In the "days are long but years are short" stage of life, or when watching a loved one's body be ravaged by an unrelenting terminal illness, or in the depths of despair when the dream of what your life would be is shattered, the possibility of joy can feel unimaginable. Believing in beauty coming out of ashes or a shoot growing from the stump seem like foolish hopes.

Even when it seems that there is no change, things do not remain the same. God continues to come near. Sometimes God is revealed through angel choirs or calmed storms, and sometimes in the ministrations of a good Samaritan, or in treasured words to ponder. Transformation comes in a million different ways. Sometimes it comes as order to chaos, streams in the desert, and manna from heaven. Sometimes it comes as yeast, parables, and breaking bread together. But it seems that no matter what form it takes, it is always surprising.

Like the shepherds, we too long for confirmation of the promise. We set out, leaving our ordinary, comfortable, and familiar ways in search of evidence of God's presence.

Christmas is a season of revolution as we remember and celebrate God's coming to us in this way. This seismic change began with an angel visit. This upheaval began mustard seed small as Mary nurtured life within her. The subversion, restoration, and fulfillment of proclamation, prophecy, and poetry had to grow up from baby to boy to man. And this man taught and loved. Jesus gathered and scattered. He told stories filled with challenge as he remembered and retold God's story. Jesus wrote the next chapter through suffering, death, and resurrection. And the world changed. And the world is changing.

After all this preparation and waiting, the world is now forever changed by the incarnation. And so, too, are our individual lives. Just as circumstances can turn on a dime and our lives are forever changed in tragic ways, so, too, the miracle can arrive, transformation can come, and the seed can sprout into bloom. Sometimes slow, sometimes dramatic, but always, change comes.

## BLESSING FOR WAITING

In the midst of troubled times,
  we are waiting—

In the reflection and celebration,
  we are waiting—

In the pain of grief and loss,
  we are waiting—

  for peace,
  for clarity,
  for relief,
  we are waiting.

And in this time of holy waiting,
  may we experience
  the growing light,
  the inbreaking of hope,
  and the renewal of healing,

  for we are waiting.

*December 24*

# LIGHT

LECTIONARY READING: JOHN 1:1–14

In the beginning was the Word, and the Word was with God, and the Word was God. He was in the beginning with God. All things came into being through him, and without him not one thing came into being. What has come into being in him was life, and the life was the light of all people. The light shines in the darkness, and the darkness did not overtake it. **(John 1:1–5)**

Our Advent journey now brings us to Christmas Eve. The familiar carols and artistic renderings of that holy scene conjure images of a still and peaceful night. We hear the words of Scripture and sing the refrains that proclaim great joy, of being chosen, of miracles, and of angels. In the familiarity of these traditions and the fear and pain of our grievous present, we may forget that the messiah's arrival, a newborn king, and an upside-down kingdom are good news, especially for those who are oppressed and suffering.

Part of the intensity of pain during the holidays is our reckoning with the reality that we only ever truly have the present moment. In our efforts to avoid or numb our discomfort, some of us look to the future. We plan and prepare; we anticipate and dream. Others of us fixate on the past, either with rose-colored glasses and such nostalgia that the present could never live up to what was, or with regret, longing, and a sigh of "if only." These mindsets keep us from where we can actually have an impact: the present moment. Perhaps when Jesus speaks of not worrying about tomorrow (Matthew 6:25–34), it is more than a command or promise of future provision—but instead an invitation to be attentive to what is, as it is.

Throughout Scripture, the admonition "Fear not!" rings out. It seems that a common response to a divine encounter or invitation is fear and concern, not the comforting blessing we assume it will be and long for in our own circumstances. This is a challenge for those of us on unchosen journeys, those who know longing, who are suffering.

Hardened hearts in the face of fear are a reasonable, expected response. Our bodies are trying to protect us. Yet we see the truth throughout the Christmas story: those who were closed off, content, or assured were the ones who missed the miracle. God worked through those who were willing to say yes to the divine invitation. Elizabeth and Zechariah, Mary and Joseph, and the shepherds and magi, all participated in the miracle of the incarnation through their openness, responsiveness, and curiosity.

Receiving the gift of God's presence does require something of us. Our honest accounting of what has happened, our deepest longings, and our fears and pains, can all be laid before God. As it was in the beginning, with Word and wisdom hovering over the chaos, so too these gifts, the *logos* (word) and *sophia* (wisdom)—the very presence of God's Spirit—are celebrated with the incarnation (see John 1:1–5; Luke 1:35, 41; Matthew 1:18–19). We must stay soft, holding on to hope, open to the possibility of transformation, eyes peeled for the spark of light, attentive and present to what is happening right here, right now.

This Christmas Eve, may we invite wisdom and the Word to meet us in our chaos and longing. May we invite the incarnation to be revealed in our own hearts and lives, and may we join with all those who bore witness to the birth of Jesus in wonder. Our soft hearts, our posture of hope, prepare us to wonder at God's goodness, faithful and surprising, which arrives at the margins of our lives in ways we never imagined or expected.

## BLESSING FOR LIGHT

It is a beginning,
    and perhaps it is as it was in the beginning,
    chaotic, formless . . .
And perhaps there is darkness,
    but not darkness that can overcome the spark.

So may you,
    receiving and believing,
    now a child of God,
    experience grace upon grace.

For as it was in the beginning,
    the Word was with God, just as you always are.

And as it was in the beginning,
    the life, being, and light that gives light to the world
    is with everyone,
    and is for everyone.

*December 25*

# CHRISTMAS

LECTIONARY READING: COLOSSIANS 1:15–20

---

For in him all the fullness of God was pleased to dwell, and through him God was pleased to reconcile to himself all things, whether on earth or in heaven, by making peace through the blood of his cross. **(Colossians 1:19–20)**

---

The rhythms of the church year now move us into Christmastide. It's a reminder that the only constant is change. Things will not always be like this. Time may not heal all things, but time and space do give perspective. We are not untouched by all that swirls around us.

The Christmas story is full of ordinary folks caught up in God's extraordinary actions. Luke records Mary, Joseph, Herod, Zechariah, Elizabeth, John, Simeon, Anna, the shepherds, and the angels, not just providing a play-by-play or plot summary, but giving us a window into the impact of the incarnation on a wide variety of people. Each had their own griefs and struggles, worries and wonderings. Each was affected by this invitation and arrival in different ways. Each experienced God with fear and wonder.

No matter what feeling is stirred in us today, Scripture reminds us that those caught up in the unfolding drama of the nativity also had a wide range of experiences. There is space for fear and great joy, for grief and wild hope. Regardless of how you feel or what you are facing this Christmas, there is good news. The words of Scripture, written long ago, demonstrate again and again: God is at work. God is present. God is always surprising, moving, and making something new.

The good tidings and great joy proclaimed then and now is the gift of Emmanuel. God has come to be with us in the flesh. This with-ness is at the heart of Christmas. This good news first came to those on the margins. God revealed to ordinary folks. God invites those without power and position to first receive and then to be the messengers of good news.

So, in a weary world and with fragile hope, we celebrate Christmas. For those of us on the margins of celebration or society, for those of us who feel overlooked or forgotten in this season, the Savior comes. We are invited to embrace the gift of Emmanuel, God with us, in the midst of whatever we are facing.

Christmas is not the finale or a resolution. In fact, the very definition of *advent* is a beginning, the start of something new in the world. And so today we also remember and celebrate that Jesus' birth is just one part of the story. There is more to come. It is good news, yet it is not the whole of the story. The full implications of the incarnation are yet to be revealed in the life, ministry, death, and resurrection of Jesus.

From creation to the nativity, from crucifixion to Pentecost, from the time of the early church gatherings to today, God is proclaiming *I have always been present. I have always been near. I am here. I am with you.*

In this season, may we tenderly hold this wonder and mystery. May we notice the gift of God's presence with us in all things, and may we claim the promise of God's continued goodness and grace as we navigate the realities of the already and not yet. We live in hope and anticipation that God's shalom is somehow enough, that the fullness of God's dwelling, in which all things hold together and find reconciliation, is for us. It is the spark of light that the dark cannot overcome. Thanks be to God.

## BLESSING FOR CHRISTMAS

From the beginning
  and in the beginning,
  God has been
  Emmanuel—God with us.

And the fullness of God
  dwells in Christ Jesus.

On this day of celebrating
  the incarnation,
  may you sense the nearness of God,
  who was made visible in Jesus
  and is visible through God's beloved.

From the beginning
  and in the beginning,
  we have reflected the divine image
  Emmanuel—God with us.

And reconciliation
  comes through Christ Jesus.

On this day of celebrating
  the incarnation,
  may you abide in the peace of Christ,
  for in him, all things hold together,
  and with him, you are held.

Now and forevermore.
May it be so.

# CONCLUSION

Arise, shine, for your light has come,
 and the glory of the LORD has risen upon you.
For darkness shall cover the earth
 and thick darkness the peoples,
but the LORD will arise upon you,
 and his glory will appear over you.
Nations shall come to your light
 and kings to the brightness of your dawn. **(Isaiah 60:1–3)**

Technically, the celebration of Christmas continues after December 25. The twelve days of Christmas, also known as Christmastide, have traditionally been the time for carol singing and feasting, concluding on January 5. In my community, the Amish mark "Old Christmas" with a celebration on January 6, the Feast of Epiphany. The tradition of exchanging gifts finds roots in this story of honoring the arrival of the magi with their gifts for the newborn king.

We may forget that the good news of Jesus' birth came during difficult circumstances. Our celebrations and traditions may omit the context of the magi visit. Horror continues in the unfolding story of God with us. Christ's coming does not immediately resolve the tensions and troubles of the times. The nativity is one more chapter of this grand story. So, too, our grief, pain, and longing may not be cured or resolved as we conclude the holiday season.

The liturgical celebration of Epiphany often gets bypassed with our move into the new year. With the feast day of Christmas past, holiday trappings are packed away. We start thinking about resolutions and goals. Those of us in the Northern Hemisphere prepare for the last long weeks of winter, now devoid of the swirl of activities and anticipation.

So really, it is an appropriate time to consider and honor Epiphany in a season that invites us to slow down, rest, and perhaps hibernate. Nature's rhythms remind us that fallow times are necessary, that periods of dormancy bring growth. We are now invited to a different kind of waiting.

The rhythms of the church year invite us to stay alert for signs of light and life. As we reflect on the past month, we can pay attention to where we may have noticed a brightening or a sign of change. What are we hopeful for in the coming days?

Throughout Advent, we have made our preparations. We have honed our skills for waiting, noticing, and anticipating. As we turn the page on the calendar to a new year, we are invited to mark Epiphany, a celebration of the arriving light.

The word *epiphany* means an appearance or manifestation, specifically of a deity. But it can also signify a sudden insight or intuitive perception. In mid to late winter, we look for the signs of illumination and revelation relating to the wonderings and worries we hold. This is now the season for honoring what has happened in the hiddenness of the dark, even as we welcome the dawn and notice growth, newness, and transformation. We can name where we have experienced the nearness of God recently.

Epiphany connects us to the ongoing story of God. We bear witness to the light that has come and notice where the light shines on. We join the long line of light bearers following in the way of Jesus, holding on to hope for redemption, restoration, and the revealing of shalom in all places for all people.

## BLESSING FOR A NEW YEAR

In the depths of winter,
  an awakening—
  Epiphany!

A prophecy and call,
  an invitation and promise—
  light and sight—
  Epiphany!

What you await arrives,
  from the formless, an unveiling—
  Epiphany!

Unforced yet compelled,
  vision and clarity.
As it all comes together,
  a glow of deep joy
  Blessed abundance—
  Epiphany!

# BONUS MATERIALS

# ADAPTING FOR SMALL GROUPS

Community is a core value of Anabaptism. Just as the two walking on the road to Emmaus recognized the presence of Jesus with them as they discussed what they were wondering and experiencing (Luke 24:13–35), Anabaptists believe that through reading Scripture together, joining in prayer for one another, and sharing about our lives, the Spirit of God is revealed. Our discipleship is shaped by the insight and accountability that we experience in community.

While this devotional was envisioned for individual use, it can also be adapted for small group discussion during the Christmas season. You may wish to offer a one-day or evening retreat at the start of Advent, or you may gather with a small group weekly for conversation and contemplation.

For weekly gatherings, plan forty-five minutes to an hour for the group to work through the material. Of course, you can always add or extend time for quiet reflection or journaling to fit your schedule. Suggested arrangements for the content can be adapted based on how frequently your group meets.

*Option 1:* Select one devotional to use as the framework for the discussion.

*Option 2:* Select the devotional that focuses on the scripture text for worship this week. Consult with your pastor or worship planner to determine which texts will be the focus for worship throughout the Sundays in Advent. For easy reference, scripture indexes are included on page 133.

*Option 3:* If you are meeting weekly during the five weeks of Advent and Christmas, discuss five devotionals per session.

*Option 4:* Beginning with the invitation (p. 17), read each reflection aloud. Offer opportunities for comments or discussion. When a natural conclusion is reached, move on to the next daily devotional. Simply move through the material at the pace of the group's interest. You may spend more time on particular passages or themes.

Regardless of which option you choose, consider these guidelines for setting the tone and guiding the conversation.

**WELCOME |** Offer a clear opening time for the gathering. Be sure everyone is acquainted. You may choose to offer an opportunity for check-ins, sharing, or prayer requests so that everyone has a sense of what people are carrying as they enter into this time. Participation is easier for people if they have had a chance to engage in the opening time.

Additionally, you could include a ritual of candle lighting, either using your own words of welcome and prayer or drawing from one of the litanies (pp. 116–26) as a way of beginning the discussion.

**READING SCRIPTURE |** Have someone from the group read the scripture text of the selected devotional. It may be helpful to read the entire lectionary text, not just the verses highlighted in this book, as it will give more context to the text and theme that you will be reflecting on.

You may wish to engage in the spiritual practice of *lectio divina* (divine reading). To do this, read the passage aloud* three times, allowing for silence between each reading. The same person or multiple people may read aloud. Invite everyone to listen, paying attention to words or phrases that stand out each time. The text should be read in a slow and thoughtful way. Offer an opportunity for people to share what they noticed, wondered about, or connected with in their own life.

Variations on reading aloud could include offering a printout of the text for people to mark up and jot notes on. Hearing the text read in different versions or translations can also provide interesting prompts for reflection.

**REFLECTION |** Read the reflection for the chosen day aloud. Invite people to respond to the questions, themes, and personal reflections the devotional stirred in them. What resonates for them? What challenges them? Where are they noticing God? What will they take with them this week?

Depending on the time and interests of the group, everyone could write their own blessing or prayer for the week, drawing on the scripture reading, devotional, and their group conversation.

**BLESSING |** Offer the blessing for the day (or choose one from the selections) to close your time of conversation.

# ADAPTING FOR USE IN WORSHIP

*Option 1:* Choose one of the daily devotionals to focus the worship service on. You may draw from the introduction and opening invitation (pp. 11–20) to shape the opening remarks of the gathering. Use one of the candle-lighting litanies (pp. 116–26) as a ritual within the service. The devotional can be the prompt for reflection and a sermon starter based on the chosen scripture text and theme. Use the correlating blessing as the benediction or sending element of the service.

*Option 2:* Drawing on the format of the Longest Night Service (p. 127), use the scripture texts and blessings of your choice to shape the service. For the time of gathering/invitation, choose a set of candle-lighting litanies (pp. 116–26) to use each week. Alternate Advent and Christmas hymns with the daily scripture readings from the days leading up to that Sunday. You may want to offer one to three of the passages for contemplation. Use one of the blessings (connected to the scripture texts you chose) as the sending blessing for the service.

*Option 3:* For smaller groups or non-traditional worship gatherings, consider using the format for Adapting for Small Groups (p. 109) to shape the service. Advent and Christmas songs could be included between the gathering time and before the blessing. Select a candle-lighting litany (pp. 116–26) from the included material to use in the time of gathering or as a call to worship.

# ADVENT CANDLE-LIGHTING LITANIES

During the season of Advent, some congregations participate in a ritual of lighting candles, often using an Advent wreath. Some households also adopt this practice as part of their celebrations at home. The following candle-lighting litanies can be used congregationally (as part of a call to worship, as a response to the sermon, or as its own element of the service), at home, or in small-group settings.

Traditionally, the Advent wreath holds four candles, one for each week, with a Christ candle in the center. The Christ candle is lit on Christmas Eve or at the Christmas service. Often, the themes of Advent remain the same each year: love, joy, peace, and hope. Each week an additional candle is lit, increasing the light as we move toward Christmas. While churches may represent this in a variety of ways, traditionally, the Advent candles display three different colors of candles. There are three purple candles (for hope, peace, and love), one pink candle (for joy), and one white candle (for Christ).

These litanies may be read in parts, as they were originally written for two voices. However, reading the reflections congregationally in unison or by a single worship leader will also be effective. For public offerings, it works well to practice reading these aloud ahead of time for clarity and pacing. These may also be adapted with lines for the congregation or gathered group to voice.

*Advent candle lighting*

# KEEPING TIME

## WEEK 1

The ritual of Advent candle lighting reminds us that we are on a different timetable than the world.

*There are plenty of calendars that shape our lives—*
*school calendars, fiscal year calendars, and national calendars, all of them with their own values and concerns.*

The Christian calendar focuses on the life of Christ and what his life tells us about our own lives with God.

*Week by week we will light new candles as a reminder and as a sign.*

We know and believe the light has come.
The light will come.
But it will not be rushed.

*Our job is to wait without losing hope.*

So today we light a candle—
as a sign of our hope in the coming of the light that the darkness cannot overcome.

## WEEK 2

The ritual of Advent candle lighting reminds us that we are on a different timetable than the world.

*The Christian calendar focuses on the life of Christ and what his life tells us about our own lives with God.*

We know and believe the light has come.

*Our job is to wait without losing hope.*

So today we light a candle—
as a sign of our hope in the coming of the light that the darkness cannot overcome.

*Today we light a second candle—*
*as a sign of the gift of peace that God has promised to God's people.*

## WEEK 3

The ritual of Advent candle lighting reminds us that we are on a different timetable than the world.

*We know and believe the light has come.*
*And our job is to wait without losing hope.*

So today we light a candle—
as a sign of our hope in the coming of the light that the darkness cannot overcome.

*Today we light a second candle—*
*as a sign of the gift of peace that God has promised to God's people.*

Today, we light a third candle—
as a sign of the joy that comes with the promise of restoration.

## WEEK 4

The ritual of Advent candle lighting reminds us that we are on a different timetable than the world.

*We know and believe the light has come.*
*And our job is to wait without losing hope.*

So today we light a candle—
as a sign of our hope in the coming of the light that the darkness cannot overcome.

*Today we light a second candle—*
*as a sign of the gift of peace that God has promised to God's people.*

Today, we light a third candle—
as a sign of the joy that comes with the promise of restoration.

*Today, we light a fourth candle—*
*as a sign of God's faithfulness.*

## WEEK 5

The ritual of Advent candle lighting reminds us that we are on a different timetable than the world.

*We know and believe the light has come.*
*And our job is to wait without losing hope.*

So today we light a candle—
as a sign of our hope in the coming of the light that the darkness cannot overcome.

*Today we light a second candle—*
*as a sign of the gift of peace that God has promised to God's people.*

Today, we light a third candle—
as a sign of the joy that comes with the promise of restoration.

*Today, we light a fourth candle—*
*as a sign of God's faithfulness.*

And, we now light the Christ candle as a sign of God's presence, dwelling among us.

## WEEK 6

The ritual of Advent candle lighting reminds us that we are on a different timetable than the world.

*Today we celebrate Epiphany—marking the end of our journey through Advent and the celebrations of incarnation and Christmas.*

In Epiphany, we mark the coming of the magi and the sharing of the good news—
the expanding presence of the light that has come in Christ.

*Epiphany reminds us that the light continues to spread—beyond the stable, beyond Bethlehem, and into the whole world.*

We know and believe the light has come. And now our job is to share that good news—to shine the light into all places.

*So today, we light our Advent candles,*
*remembering the signs of hope, peace, joy, and faithfulness.*

And we light the Christ candle as a sign of God's presence, dwelling among us.

*Advent candle lighting*

## THE PEOPLE OF ADVENT

### WEEK 1

God of Advent, in the darkest days and nights of the year,
*our hearts turn toward your promised light.*

With the first faint glimmer of a single candle—
*our hope is ignited once more.*

In these Advent days,
lead us into your light,
to a manger where the face of God shines bright and clear.
*We join with those who receive the gift of Emmanuel.*

Today we join our voices with the angels—who foretold, who bore witness, and who proclaimed in chorus:
*Glory to God in the highest.*
*Glory to God in the highest.*
*Glory to God in the highest.*

We join with those who receive him—
the gift of Emmanuel, the gift of you,
God, with us.
Amen.

## WEEK 2

God of Advent, in the darkest days and nights of the year,
*our hearts turn toward your promised light.*

With the first faint glimmer of a single candle,
dancing into the light of many bright flames,
*our hope is ignited once more.*

In these Advent days,
lead us into your light,
to a manger where the face of God shines bright and clear.
*We join with those who receive the gift of Emmanuel.*

Today we join our voices with the shepherds—
who were surprised and frightened and then amazed:
*Let us go now!*
*Let us see this thing the Lord has made known to us.*
*Let us glorify and praise our great God!*

We join with those who receive him—
the gift of Emmanuel, the gift of you,
God, with us.
Amen.

## WEEK 3

God of Advent, in the darkest days and nights of the year,
    *our hearts turn toward your promised light.*

With the first faint glimmer of a single candle,
    dancing into the light of many bright flames,
    *our hope is ignited once more.*

In these Advent days,
    lead us into your light,
    to a manger where the face of God shines bright and clear.
*We join with those who receive the gift of Emmanuel.*

Today we join our voices with Bethlehem—
    who hosted and held space,
    who connected history and the future.

*We remember your acts in this space.*
*We rejoice in your presence now.*
*We anticipate the goodness to come.*

We join with those who receive him—
    the gift of Emmanuel, the gift of you,
    God, with us.
Amen.

## WEEK 4

God of Advent,
in the darkest days and nights of the year,
*our hearts turn toward your promised light.*

With the first faint glimmer of a single candle,
dancing into the light of many bright flames,
*our hope is ignited once more.*

In these Advent days,
lead us into your light,
to a manger where the face of God shines bright and clear.
*We join with those who receive the gift of Emmanuel.*

Today we proclaim that we, too, are part of those who receive the good news.
We join with those who receive him—
the gift of Emmanuel, the gift of you,
God, with us.
Amen.

## WEEK 5

God of Advent, in the darkest days and nights of the year,
*our hearts turn toward your promised light.*

With the first faint glimmer of a single candle,
dancing into the light of many bright flames,
*our hope is ignited once more.*

In this Christmas season,
lead us into your light,
to a manger where the face of God shines bright and clear.
*We join with those who receive the gift of Emmanuel.*

Today we join our voices with the magi—
who followed the star,
and offered their gifts,
and were overwhelmed with joy.
*Joy to the world!*
*Joy to the world!*
*Joy to the world!*

We join with those who receive him—
the gift of Emmanuel, the gift of you,
God, with us.
Amen.

# BLUE CHRISTMAS

## A WORSHIP GATHERING FOR THE LONGEST NIGHT

This is a guide for creating a corporate worship experience that honors the experience of darkness. While this resource can be used by pastors and worship planners, it can also be adapted by individuals to host a gathering in their homes or as a special event with a small group, within a school community, or for those in a care facility.

In the Northern Hemisphere, winter solstice, the longest stretch of darkness, falls in December. Some Christian traditions have marked this with a time of corporate worship, a unique gathering often referred to as Longest Night or Blue Christmas. This time focuses on creating a space for those who have lost loved ones to honor their memory and grieve.

While the traditional themes of Advent worship (love, joy, peace, and hope) include opportunities to offer lament and longing, most often, Christmastide worship services are festive and cheerful. For those who are in an acute experience of grief or loss, it can be difficult to connect with God and the gathered community when their reality goes unacknowledged.

## GATHERING

*The atmosphere of this gathering is often somber. Quiet, reflective, instrumental music, simple or stark visuals, and candlelight are appropriate for setting the tone for this sacred time. A single lit candle, surrounded by unlit tapers or tealight candles, may be featured on a central table.*

## INVITATION

On this longest night of the year, we gather to acknowledge our grief. In the midst of the celebration and joy of the coming of Emmanuel, we create space for our lament. Tonight, we recognize the grief, longing, disappointment, and pain of the experiences we carry. We tenderly offer them before the true Light. We trust in the words from the gospel of John:

> *In the beginning was the Word, and the Word was with God, and the Word was God. He was in the beginning with God. All things came into being through him, and without him not one thing came into being. What has come into being in him was life, and the life was the light of all people. The light shines in the darkness, and the darkness did not overtake it. (John 1:1–5)*

## INVOCATION

As we gather, O God, we remember that it is out of chaos that you create.
It is in the silence that your Word arrives.
It is into the darkness that your light shines.
It is out of death that resurrection comes.
May your loving presence draw near to us in this season of waiting.
Amen.

## SCRIPTURE AND SONGS

*As the group may be small, or the gathering may be emotional, it may be more appropriate to have music accompanied or offered by an ensemble. Alternating between reading scripture and singing can create a space for reflection and comfort. Feel free to select from among these options or use multiple songs between readings.*

| SONG POSSIBILITIES | SUGGESTED SCRIPTURE TEXTS |
|---|---|
| **"O Come, O Come, Emmanuel"**<br>**"Longing for Light"** | *Isaiah 26:16–18* |
| **"Comfort, Comfort, O My People"**<br>**"We Come"** | *Psalm 71:4–11* |
| **"O God, Our Help in Ages Past"**<br>**"In the Quiet Curve of Evening"** | *Micah 4:5–10* |
| **"Move in Our Midst"**<br>**"Abide with Me"** | *Romans 8:18–25* |
| **"Come, Thou Long-Expected Jesus"**<br>**"Helpless and Hungry"** | *Isaiah 11:1–11* |

## CANDLE LIGHTING

*Offer an opportunity for participants to come forward and light a candle to mark their grief. The candle may represent a loved one, a loss from this past year, or a simple acknowledgment that this is a difficult time. It would also be appropriate for the worship leader or pastor to light a candle and name those from the congregation or community who have died within the last year. This can be a time of silent action; providing instrumental music is also an option.*

Tonight, we light candles to mark this holy time and space.
Each of us is invited to come forward and participate.
The candles we light on this longest night represent the grief, loss, and pain that we carry in this Advent season.

Candle lighting is our offering and petition before God.
We invite the Holy Comforter to draw near.
We ask the Spirit of God to carry what we cannot.
We plead with the One who was, who is, and who is to come, to bring restoration and reconciliation, renewal and refreshment—to be a beacon of light in our longest night.

O God, as we light these candles, may we remember that your light shines and the darkness will not overtake it. Amen.

*Reverent time of reflection and candle lighting.*

*This time may be concluded with a song such as "Longing for Light" or "We Come."*

## SENDING BLESSING

May you dare to hope—
when you find yourself in darkness
staring down into the deep,
facing the swirl of chaos.

May you have the courage to step up
to the precipice, a threshold,
to teeter on the edge.

May you dare to hope—
when you feel the sweep of the Wind,
hear the whisper of the Divine,
notice the pinprick of Light.

May you have the patience to
sit in the before, on the threshold,
holding on through the not-quite-yet.

May you dare to hope,
for in the
wind and waves,
darkness and light,
chaos and order,

God has come,
and
God is not done.

# SCRIPTURE INDEXES

# ACKNOWLEDGMENTS

I am thankful for the people who have vulnerably shared their experiences with me. In spiritual direction, pastoral care, and friendship, I have borne witness to the bleak midwinter. Entering into this tender and sacred space has been a gift, and I pray the reflections and offerings here gently companion others through a difficult season.

Deepest gratitude to Tiana, whose kind encouragement sparked the idea to create a book that centered blessings, along with the kismet of Amy's offhanded comment, which led to the revival of the idea for this Advent guide. However, it was Sara Versluis whose keen eye, gentle nudges, and confidence motivated me to move this from concept to words on the page. Thank you!

Everyone needs good friends and a community of support, and I have an embarrassment of riches when it comes to this kind of connection and care. Thank you, Beth Hofstetter Falb, Jen Steiner, and Jolene Jaquet, for your texts, "polos," and coffee dates of celebration and encouragement. The faithful, tenacious, and steadfast encouragement and confidence of Dawn Monger has been invaluable; thank you for caring about every nuance, listening to the whole messy process, and being the counterpoint to my inner critic.

Thanks to my collaborator on the blog *Some Comfort and Joy*, Gwen Lantz, whose partnership has been instrumental in getting to this place. I love the book we created together, and through our conversations and writing, I realized I had (even) more to say about Advent.

There aren't enough words to express my appreciation for my family's sacrifice and support. In particular, Doug, Miriam, Charissa, and Maria, who pored over every word, made space for me to write, and offered kind encouragement along the way. And to BJ, Anna, and

Titus, who cheerfully backed this endeavor. You made pursuing this project possible.

I am indebted to the Herald Press team, including Amy Gingerich, Elisabeth Ivey, Sara Versluis, Bethany Barnett, Alyssa Bennett Smith, and LeAnn Hamby. You have helped make a dream come true.

# NOTES

1. See Christine Valters Paintner, *The Love of Thousands: How Angels, Saints and Ancestors Walk with Us towards Holiness* (Sorin Books, 2023), 91.
2. Wilda C. Gafney, *Womanist Midrash, Volume 2: A Reintroduction to the Women of Joshua, Judges, Samuel, and Kings* (Westminster John Knox, 2024), 3–12.
3. Tish Harrison Warren, *Prayer in the Night: For Those Who Work or Watch or Weep* (InterVarsity Press, 2021), 60.
4. See Jenai Auman, *Othered: Finding Belonging with the God Who Pursues the Hurt, Harmed, and Marginalized* (Baker, 2024).
5. See, e.g., James H. Waltner, *Psalms*, Believers Church Bible Commentary (Herald Press, 2006), 380.
6. Wilda C. Gafney, *A Women's Lectionary for the Whole Church Year A* (Church Publishing Incorporated, 2021), 11.
7. Gafney, *Womanist Midrash, Volume* 2, 136.
8. Gafney, *Womanist Midrash, Volume* 2, 138.
9. Warren, *Prayer in the Night*, 50.
10. See Waltner, *Psalms*, 334.
11. Frank E. Gaebelein, *Psalms*, Expositor's Bible Commentary (Zondervan, 2008), 43.
12. Kathleen Norris, *The Cloister Walk* (Riverhead Books, 1996), 96.
13. Warren, *Prayer in the Night*, 52.
14. Warren, *Prayer in the Night*, 119.
15. Christine Valters Paintner, *Birthing the Holy: Wisdom from Mary to Nurture Creativity and Renewal* (Sorin Books, 2022), XVII.
16. Warren, *Prayer in the Night*, 29.
17. See Wendy Wright, *Sacred Dwelling: A Spirituality of Family Life* (Forest of Peace Books, 1994), 114–19.
18. Scott Erickson, interviewed by Jen Hatmaker, *For the Love*, podcast, series 64, episode 19, "Scott Erickson Paints an Honest Picture of an Advent Season of Hope," December 11, 2024.
19. Stephanie Duncan Smith, *Even After Everything: The Spiritual Practice of Knowing the Risks and Loving Anyway* (Convergent, 2024), 50.

# THE AUTHOR

Sherah-Leigh Gerber is a spiritual director and writer. A graduate of Eastern Mennonite Seminary and an ordained minister in Mennonite Church USA, Gerber has served as a pastor in addition to working in other nonprofit leadership roles. Gerber lives with her husband and two teenage children on a fifth-generation farm in northeastern Ohio. She is the coauthor of *Comfort and Joy: Readings and Practices for Advent*. You can learn more about her work at SherGerber.com.

"This is the real-life Advent devotional I've been waiting for. Sherah-Leigh Gerber's reflective, stripped-down theology leaves room for everyday peril amid the twinkle lights. May this honest guide be our reminder that Emmanuel showed up, stuck around, and journeys with us in our doubt, our grief, and our ordinary bliss."

**SHANNAN MARTIN**, author of *Start with Hello* and *The Ministry of Ordinary Places*

"Advent is my favorite season of the year, but it is not always an emotionally easy season. If we hold space for the true nature of the waiting of Advent, it's a countercultural time for the unknown and even the unhappy. But as the angel said, "Do not be afraid," for this lovely book holds reflections and blessings to accompany you through all the days of waiting that Advent brings."

**WHITNEY R. SIMPSON**, author of *With God in Every Breath: A Guide to Drawing Closer to Jesus through Your Senses*

"Sherah-Leigh Gerber clearly loves Advent, not only as a lead-in to the main event of Christmas, but as a season of honest reflection and deep longing, a season for waiting on God and being surprised by unexpected blessings. This is a book to savor: with readings from Scripture, daily reflections and words of blessing, and bonus materials to use this book with a small group or in a worship setting."

**APRIL YAMASAKI**, pastor and author of *Hope Beyond Our Sorrows* and *Sacred Pauses*

"A refreshingly honest and unique Advent devotional. Sherah-Leigh Gerber readily admits that all is not merry and bright. Not for us, nor for those who first sat in darkness, longing for the Messiah to break in to their realities of fear, disappointment, oppression and death. If you're struggling to find joy this Christmas season, *Unhappy Holidays* will speak tender words of comfort to your weary soul."

**JASON PORTERFIELD**, author of *Fight Like Jesus: How Jesus Waged Peace throughout Holy Week*

"*Unhappy Holidays* is the book we all need at some point in our journey. As a therapist, I value this resource as a gentle companion for anyone struggling through the holidays for a variety of reasons that the reader may not be able to articulate. This book is a great gift for the person who meets the holidays with grief, loss, or ambivalence."

**BRENDA L. YODER**, licensed mental health counselor and author of *Uncomplicated: Simple Secrets for a Compelling Life*

"I know very few people who feel 'merry' around the holidays. Most, though, long to engage with the One who is intimately familiar with the lives they lead and the challenges they face. If that's you—and I suspect it is—I hope you'll welcome *Unhappy Holidays* as the new holiday tradition that will bless you and the ones you love."

**MARGOT STARBUCK**, *New York Times* bestselling writer and author of *The Solid Place: 365 Affirmations for Thriving Emotionally and Spiritually*

"*Unhappy Holidays* somehow recounts the familiar Advent journey where the darkness of grief meets the light of grace with honesty and comfort. As a pastor honoring the spirit of waiting, Sherah-Leigh Gerber captures the slow moves of God in this season of unfolding. Her ordinary but parabolic stories are like the bread and wine of communion that meet us in our unique Advent locations and fill us up with the richness of having been with God. This book resources a sacred Advent with extra prompts to use in worshiping communities of many sizes, ensuring we don't journey alone."

**SHANNON W. DYCUS**, author of *The Holy in the Night: Finding Freedom in a Season of Waiting*

"*Unhappy Holidays* invites us to live into the beautiful complexity of Advent rather than succumb to the cheerful veneer of the secular holiday season. In her gentle weaving of the biblical story with our contemporary stories, Sherah-Leigh Gerber creates a nurturing space for those who carry grief with them into this holy season."

**JOANNA HARADER**, author of *Prone to Wander* and *Expecting Emmanuel*